THE
GODDESS
ORACLE

AMY SOPHIA MARASHINSKY, author, drummer, ceremonialist and "kitchen witch" facilitates intense workshops and circles that weave a web of safe, transformational space. Featured in a *Harper's Bazaar* article on the Goddess, she is also an award-winning filmmaker, writer, director and producer of theater, and has written for radio in Japan. Marashinsky has also appeared on many radio stations and has released a drumming album, *Rhythms from the Womb,* and an album of lyrical monologues of Greek Goddesses, *The Goddess Perspective*. She was co-editor (with Susun Weed) of *Luna Yoga: Vital Fertility and Sexuality,* by Adelheid Ohlig. She is available for workshops and intuitive readings from *The Goddess Oracle,* and conducts Shamanic-Priestess Apprenticeships which focus on the path to wholeness. Marashinsky is currently working on her next book, "Deep Nourishment: The Art of Magical Cooking."

HRANA JANTO is an artist who has long inhabited the realms of history, fantasy, myth and the Sacred. Her commissioned works include paintings for the Bill Moyers' PBS series "Joseph Campbell and the Power of Myth." Her art has graced many book covers, including the Chelsea House series Monsters of Mythology, and her work on the 1992–95 calendars, *The Goddess* and *Magic and Myth* is legendary. Janto's work has also appeared in magazines such as *New York Daily News, Bellcore* and *Cricket,* and on a poster for a Miramax film. She has exhibited throughout New York, New England and California, including pieces at the Books of Wonder Gallery and a Society of Illustrators show. Her works are currently shown through the Elizabeth Stone Gallery in Birmingham, Michigan. Painting Goddesses has been her long-time passion, and the paintings in this deck represent six years of artwork. Janto lives, paints and dances in New York's Hudson Valley.

    Amy Sophia Marashinsky and Hrana Janto can be reached at:
        c/o Element Books
        160 North Washington Street
        Boston, MA 02114

THE GODDESS ORACLE

A Way to Wholeness through the Goddess and Ritual

Amy Sophia Marashinsky

ILLUSTRATED BY

Hrana Janto

E L E M E N T
Boston, Massachusetts • Shaftesbury, Dorset
Melbourne, Victoria

© 1997 Element Books, Inc.
Text © 1997 Amy Sophia Marashinsky
Artwork © 1997 Hrana Janto

First published in the USA in 1997 by
Element Books, Inc.
160 North Washington Street, Boston, MA 02114

Published in Great Britain in 1997 by
Element Books Limited
Shaftesbury, Dorset SP7 8BP

Published in Australia in 1997 by
Element Books and distributed by
Penguin Books Australia Limited
487 Maroondah Highway, Ringwood, Victoria 3134

All rights reserved. No part of this book may be reproduced or utilized,
in any form or by any means, electronic or mechanical, without prior
permission in writing from the publisher.

Text design/composition by Paperwork
Cover design by Paperwork
Printed and bound in Hong Kong

Library of Congress Cataloging-in-Publication Data

Marashinsky, Amy Sophia.
      The goddess oracle: a way to wholeness through the goddess and
ritual / written by Amy Sophia Marashinsky ; artwork by Hrana Janto.
      p.   cm.
  Includes bibliographical references.
  ISBN: 1-85230-864-8 (pbk.: alk. paper)
  1. Oracles. 2. Goddess religion. 3. Women—Religious life.
I. Title.
BF1773.M34 1997   97-166
133.3'248—dc21   CIP

British Library Cataloguing in Publication data available.

ISBN 1-85230-864-8

10 9 8 7 6 5 4

CONTENTS

Acknowledgments vii

Preface ix

Introduction xv

Visiting the Oracle xix

PART ONE: *Using the Goddess Oracle* 1

    1. Ritual 3

    2. Invoking the Oracle 8

    3. The Spreads 11

PART TWO: *The Goddesses* 19

PART THREE: *The Cards* 181

Bibliography 186

I dedicate this book with honor, respect, and love to my friends

CHARLES LAWRENCE
and
SUSUN S. WEED

teachers, mentors, courageous and fierce path walkers.

*For your work in this world, for your love of life,
for your dance of wholeness.
I thank you for inspiring me and for being part of my dance
on this earth plane.*

—AMY SOPHIA MARASHINSKY

• • •

*To the memory of my father, Martin Janto.
Your unconditional love, support, encouragement, and your
relentless strength of character still resonate within me.*

*To David Sheppard, in infinite appreciation of your integrity,
passion, and soulfulness. Thank you for all that you are
and all that you do.
I love you!*

—HRANA JANTO

ACKNOWLEDGMENTS

I WANT to begin by thanking and acknowledging the Goddesses who appear in this book. Without their willingness to speak to and through me, *The Goddess Oracle* would not exist.

Although I have spent many long hours writing *The Goddess Oracle*, the book you now hold has been made possible, made tangible, made manifest with the help, care, concern, belief, support, and nurturance of the following people: Paul Cash; Hrana Janto and Dave Sheppard; Alexandra Tait; Larry, Janie, Joshua, Sam and Isaiah Machiz; Meg White; Barbara Feldman; Lawrence Lyons; Alisa Starkweather; Barbara Scymanky; Roger Woolger; Robin and Stephen Larsen; Cynthia Bilder; Susun S. Weed; Michael Dattore; Berkana Gervais; Jana Vilner; Julie King; Judith Havrilla; Kris Papoulo; James Wanless; Thomas Cumella; Shiva and Lakota; Hollis Melton; Hans Gunther Kern; Roberta Scimone; and Skye Alexander.

Know that you all were vital, each in your way, in helping me to create this book. I hold you all in my heart with gratitude.

—*Amy Sophia Marashinsky*

THE GODDESS ORACLE

Many thanks to my communities: Dance New England, Stone Mountain Farm, Frolic Folk. Thanks to the delights and grace of Spirit inspiring these images—Thank you, Goddess! Special thanks to those who helped manifest this project: Phyllis Janto, Amy Sophia Marashinsky, Terry Buske, Chris Welles, Roberta Scimone, Paul Cash, Robin Larsen, Alexandra Tait, Sena, Bea Ehrsam, Annabelle, Jennifer, Judith and Al Havrilla, Corin, Lisa and Paul Kennedy-Spielman, Greta and Mikio, Annie Loney, Carrie Chapman, Abha, and all the women who graciously modeled for many of these paintings.

—*Hrana Janto*

PREFACE

WHY the Goddess? Do we really need another divinity, another religion, something else to worship?

If there is a male God, shouldn't there be a female Goddess too? Isn't that what creation is about—the male and female energies coming together to create new life? Without the female there can be no new life.

If human beings were created in the form of their creator, and there is only a male God, in whose image are women created? John Bradshaw says that children look to their parents to model behavior for them. If you live in a culture where there is only a male God and no Goddess, where's the model for the Feminine? How can girls learn to be women without the Goddess?

I was raised Jewish in the 50s, which means I was brought up to believe in an all-powerful God who made man in his image. Very validating for men. Feminine images, on the other hand, weren't so positive. I was taught to believe Eve was responsible for the expulsion from the Garden of Eden. Paradise was lost because of a woman, a snake, and an apple. I was told all women suffer in childbirth because of Eve. And Lilith, Adam's first wife who left him because she would not lie beneath him during sex, was considered a demon and rarely mentioned.

This view of woman as evil, as scapegoat, as temptress and seducer was not very validating for me as a young-woman-to-be. So I did what many invalidated girls do. I decided to grow up and be the best man for the job. Who wants to be a scapegoat? Who wants to be held responsible for losing paradise?

Yet although I suppressed my female nature so that I could succeed in a male world, I still had difficulty swallowing the Judeo-Christian values with which I had been raised. I could not believe that half the world was inferior because it was female, i.e., not made in God's image. I needed to find the truth.

Many years and many books later, I discovered that prior to patriarchy and the male God there was a female Goddess, whom all the peoples in the ancient world revered and honored. I discovered that there was a time when women were respected, when women were judges, lawmakers, officials, priestesses, rulers, landowners—when women had power. And I discovered that "history" is the story of a hostile takeover by the male warrior Gods of the civilization of the Goddess. Finally, I had arrived at the truth.

What my discovery did for me was validate my being female. Yes, there was/is a Goddess and I am created in her image. At last, I had discovered role models. I could do anything and be anything because it was in the scope of being a woman.

It is important for women to reclaim the Goddess—not just one Goddess, but all Goddesses. The more Goddesses we know,

PREFACE

the more we can celebrate, honor, and respect the diversity of the Feminine. If we celebrate, honor, respect the diversity of the Goddesses, then we can do it for ourselves.

Why the Goddess? Because we are women, diverse women, who need to see the Divine Feminine reflected back to us—from ourselves to our Goddesses and back to ourselves. Because all women are the Goddess, and it's time we saw ourselves that way.

After many years of connecting with the Goddess, facilitating women's empowerment workshops and circles, and conducting shamanic-priestess apprenticeships, artist Hrana Janto asked me if I would like to join her in creating a deck of Goddess cards. Her invitation came at a difficult period for me, when I was dealing with the end of a twenty-three-year intimate relationship and estrangement from my family.

As I enthusiastically dove into the project, I found myself swallowed up by grief I hadn't fully processed. My immune system broke down. I got lost in depression. I felt dismembered and weak, victimized and angry. How could I write about wholeness?

If I was going to write about the way to wholeness through the Goddess and ritual, I decided, I would have to experience it for myself, directly, firsthand. I decided to let the Goddesses help me reweave the rips in the fabric of my being. I decided to surrender.

Daily I drummed my grief (see **Coatlicue**, pp. 47–50). Health became my priority. I went deep into my darkest places and danced with those archetypal forces of grief and horror in ritual space until I heard the voice of the Goddess. It was **Kuan Yin**. She told me my puzzle was about compassion. Then **Lady of Beasts** appeared and said that relationships are not merely about pain. She was followed by **Pachamama** who promised she would always be there for me.

I mourned the ways I had been unable to take care of myself. Ways that had brought me to this place of grief. I apologized to myself for creating this challenging place and owned that I, and no one else, had created it. I continued to look at all the parts that had brought me here. Once I was able to do that, I was able to dance the healing dance of honoring the gift in the wound, a dance I am still doing.

Just when I thought I was out of the woods, I met my soulmate and got tossed back into the fire for more tempering. I was sick for four months until **Sulis** helped me heal myself.

Then the **Erinyes** explained that when my partner is in crisis, I am in crisis. I heard **Hathor** telling me to remember to give myself pleasure. **Cerridwen** spoke with me about death and rebirth. **Durga** helped me to establish clearer boundaries. They all came. All the Goddesses. As I learned from each of them, and most of all from myself, I came to the realization that I am whole.

The journey to wholeness is not an overnight affair. It is a dance of many steps, many partners, many twists and turns, many musics, many styles. It is unpredictable. And it takes as long as it needs to take.

Wholeness is all that goes into how we live our lives. How we take in life's challenges and what we do with them. Wholeness is how we dance the dance of life. Do we dance with grace and ease? or resistance and difficulty? Is our dance airy or earthy? fiery or watery?

PREFACE

The only thing predictable in life is that we're going to be challenged. This is the way we grow and evolve. How we respond and what we do with these challenges is ours to create. Wholeness begins when we recognize this and flow with it.

Wholeness is about re-membering ourselves. We cannot be whole when we've hidden aspects of ourselves in what Jung called our shadow. We cannot be whole when we find pieces of ourselves so unacceptable that we keep them in a canister labeled "Do Not Open for 10,000 years." Wholeness begins when we can call all of our pieces home—the dark and light, "good" and "bad," pleasant and unpleasant—and throw them a welcome home party.

Wholeness is about stamina. It is the ability to be flexible in the face of life's challenges. Wholeness is that space we have around us that gives us room to maneuver and find answers. Wholeness is a way of living that makes use of everything we are handed. It is a way of viewing life that is transformational and active, rather than static and passive.

The challenges to my wholeness continue and I now know they will never cease. I have learned that the desire to be whole calls forth constant challenges which I must embrace and welcome into the circle of wholeness I seek. I need those challenges to strengthen and create my wholeness. Wholeness is not a destination, but a journey of becoming.

The Goddess Oracle: A Way to Wholeness through the Goddess and Ritual is just that. It has been my way to wholeness and now I offer it to you.

—A.S.M.

INTRODUCTION

THERE have always been oracles and people have always used them. Whether it was to predict an unlucky day, to confirm one's choice of husband, to locate animals for a successful hunt, or to learn the outcome of a battle, part of the human condition is to want to know, prepare, and make safe the unknowable—the future.

The word *oracle* means "to speak." It also means "divine communication in response to a petition or request." Oracles were believed to utter their pronouncements when possessed by a divinity: the Goddess or God. These divine messages could be enigmatic and interpretation was sometimes needed. The Miko, blind shamans of northern Japan, to this day speak their oracles in archaic Japanese, which must be translated to be understood. Often the oracle chose to speak in a place where Earth's energies were especially powerful or rarified. (For example, the Oracle of Delphi of ancient Greece was on the slopes of Mt. Parnassus.)

Oracles of ancient times were delivered by priestesses who had been carefully selected and trained. The priestess would prepare for her oracular session by bathing in a sacred pond or spring. She would then dress in ritual garments and enter into a deep trance. Trance might be evoked through the use of sacred visionary herbs or direct spiritual linkage. Once in the trance, the Goddess would speak through her. Sometimes oracular communication was received in dreams. Priestesses or petitioners would sleep in a certain place, said to be filled with the presence of the Goddess or God, and gain answers to their requests through their dreams.

The Goddess Oracle was created to provide the petitioner (you) with easy access to the Goddesses. This transformational tool consists of a deck of cards and a book. You ask a question, shuffle the deck, and pick a card(s).

The Goddess Oracle consists of fifty-two Goddess portraits celebrating fifty-two inimitable ways the Divine Feminine has manifested and been worshipped in cultures around the world from the beginning of time. These fifty-two faces of the Divine Feminine portray all the beauty of the three sacred stages of life: maiden (or youth), mother (or maturity), and crone (old age).

Included are Goddesses from a wide range of world cultures, not just the Greco-Roman and European pantheon with which Westerners are familiar. The Goddesses presented here were chosen through a combination of research and direct communication, meaning I let the Goddesses themselves speak through me. They chose to express themselves in vivid, lyrical poetry, which begins each of the fifty-two Goddess sections, and opens the path to connecting with them. Then there's a brief mythological/cultural background about each Goddess to put you in touch with her

INTRODUCTION

world. Next there's an interpretation of what it means when she appears in your spread, what she is communicating to you. Finally, there's a ritual suggestion that you can use to work with the energy that particular Goddess embodies.

Each of the fifty-two Goddesses gracing *The Goddess Oracle* represents a particular aspect or energy in your life (see The Cards, pp. 182–185). Goddess knows, there are certainly more than fifty-two, but for the purposes of this book and deck there had to be a limit. These fifty-two aspects, which are common to human experience, are challenged by life. When you choose a particular card, it guides you to look at what you need to focus on in your life. When you bring this into your consciousness and work with it, you effect change. *The Goddess Oracle* is a road map that tells you where you are and what you need to get where you want to go.

The Goddess Oracle helps you get in touch with your present in a way that can help you create your future. It suggests rituals for working actively with the energy of a particular situation. When energy flows, situations can change, and change facilitates transformation. When energy is stagnant or blocked, it is hard for transformation to occur. *The Goddess Oracle* provides a way of unblocking/moving energy.

Sometimes you may feel stuck or so consumed and overtaken by your problems or situations that you neglect to nourish yourself. And sometimes you may forget that your challenges can be renamed as allies, then used to achieve wholeness. *The Goddess Oracle* is here to assist you in your quest for wholeness and to remind you that when you nurture wholeness, you can flow with the energy of any given situation. From a place of wholeness, even the future feels safe.

VISITING THE ORACLE

THE *walk up the mountain to the Temple of the Goddess is steep and it takes all my energy and almost all my concentration to climb. My heart is beating wildly with agitation. I am not old and I am not young, and I begin to sweat with the exertion. I cannot tell you what the weather is like, for I am being eaten by my problem.*

I reach the Temple and sound its gong. A priestess appears and soundlessly gestures for me to follow. She takes me inside to a place where I sit down and remove my sandals. She places a large vessel under my feet, then takes an urn and pours some fragrant, reviving water over my feet. She dries them with a towel and anoints them with pungent oil. I feel refreshed and renewed. She leads me to the outside labyrinth and salutes me as the Goddess, then turns and leaves me. Yes, I am the Goddess. I remember that now.

I enter the labyrinth, breathing deeply, walking slowly, and surrendering myself. As my being begins to unravel the knot that is my problem, I notice the day, the wind, the trees, the earth. I feel myself merging into the greater beingness that is the Goddess. Yes, I am the Goddess.

I walk the spiral path, that labyrinthine symbol for the Goddess. The smell of incense is strong as I enter the core of the labyrinth and the fumes are so dense that I can barely discern the masked figure of the Pythoness, Oracle and voice of the Goddess. As I kneel before the High Priestess, I state my problem and request an answer, knowing with utmost certainty that I will get what I need, and all will be well.

PART ONE

USING THE GODDESS ORACLE

1
RITUAL

RITUAL is the form and structure that enables your spirit to fly free. Ritual is the safe space you create that allows you to open to the deepest parts of yourself. Ritual is the magic that you do for yourself, your circle of loved ones, your community. Ritual is play.

Ritual is transformational. You begin the ritual in one state of being and end it in another. Change of consciousness is what happens and it can be major or minor. Group ritual, in order to be transformative, must involve all the participants in an active way. An effective ritual will leave you transformed; an ineffective one will bore you.

Ritual contributes to your wholeness by allowing enough safety and freedom for all the parts of yourself to be expressed. Ritual contributes to your wholeness by letting you swim and scamper with the Sacred.

The ritual suggestions listed in this book are just that: suggestions. They are all rituals that are part of what I do and have worked for me. You may use my suggestions precisely and faithfully or take from them only what feels right. Consider creating your own. Perhaps the opposite of a suggested ritual would work for you. All is offered in the spirit of inspiration. What you decide to do is up to you. The more you involve all your senses and all the parts of yourself, the deeper and more profound the results from your ritual will be.

What I have discovered after at least twelve years of research and careful deliberation is a form of doing ritual that involves several ingredients.

1. **Talking staff**—This helps you tell where you are in your life. You can't go anywhere unless you can admit and own where you are. Nothing changes until you accept that reality. How can you get to Maine if you don't know you are in New York? Attaching a name to something makes it tangible. What is tangible can then be transformed.

2. **Journey work**—This lets you reach into the unconscious. Cancer patients have used the imagery of Pac-Man figures destroying their cancer cells to help them recover. Athletes who achieve alpha states (deeply relaxed trance states) and then visualize themselves excelling at their sport improve their performance. You can facilitate transformation by using imaginative journeying techniques to get at the core of your unconscious.

3. **Dancing, drumming, singing**—This enables you to move the energy that needs to be transformed on a physical, cellular level. After working with your conscious self through the use of the talking staff, then your unconscious through journeying, you need to work next with your physical body. The more you

involve your whole self in the process, the deeper the level of transformation. Also, it's fun to dance, drum, and sing!

There is no right or wrong way to do ritual. Some elements I use in my rituals are

- creating a circle, either by envisioning it around me or by walking a path around the perimeter of the space in which the ritual is being performed;
- lighting incense or anointing myself with oil to clear the space;
- calling in the elements/directions to create sacred space, the space between the worlds;
- calling in the Goddess, the God, and whatever else needs to be called in;
- raising energy by dancing, drumming, chanting, or shamanically journeying, whichever is needed;
- sending the energy that has been raised;
- releasing the Goddess and the God;
- releasing the elements/directions;
- reopening the circle.

In ritual a circle is cast to create a sacred space within which you can work comfortably and safely. The circle seals in the powerful, positive energy of the ritual and keeps unwanted energies from intruding. To call in, invoke, or summon something (the elements or directions, the Goddess or God, for instance) means you invite it to be present. Calling in the elements/directions (archetypal forces) also helps you to define and hold sacred space, making your space or circle a safe container in which to work.

This is done with respect, honor, and love. The same is true when you release what you have called in, at the conclusion of the ritual. Gratitude is important; politely thank whomever you have invited to join you in your ritual for being there. A loving, respectful relationship with the Goddesses, Gods, and other energies and forces will ensure that they will continue working with you.

One of the most important parts of ritual is fun. Give yourself permission to create the most pleasure for yourself in your rituals. As long as no one is harmed, including yourself, anything is usable. Our patriarchal society has a hard time with fun, play, and pleasure. Just look at the billboards and commercials. They say you can only have fun if you are wearing the right clothes, driving the right car, consuming the right consumables. If you are trying to live as you've been taught, it may be hard for you to connect with real pleasure. Ritual is a safe place to connect with your pleasure, your joy, your ecstasy.

You don't need any tools for ritual, but if having them enables you to play more and connect with the magical parts of yourself, then by all means use them! Freedom is important, too. At times when I worked in very controlling environments, my morning ritual became my daily dose of freedom!

The rituals in the book are suggestions of ways to work with and transform the energy that a particular Goddess represents. Many of them are presented in the form of journeys. A journey is a deeply relaxed state, an altered state of consciousness. It differs from meditation in that rather than focusing on something such as your breath, light, or a mantra, you travel to and

RITUAL

experience an alternate reality such as the Underworld, Otherworld, Aboveworld, or another creative reality.

There are many ways to journey. You can journey kinetically (through your body) or you can journey visually, seeing everything pictorially. You can journey with sound, with your senses, or with your feelings. And you can journey in a way that is known only to you. Whatever you choose, trust that it is the best way for you. Give yourself over to your way of journeying, knowing that you will get what you need.

One phenomenon that occasionally shows up in people's journeys is the "journey police." They usually represent the authority figure aspect of a person's psyche. While journeying, they may pull you over and ask to see your right to journey. You will need to acknowledge them, thank them for sharing with you, and get right back to your journey.

Many of the journeys in this book can be done as physical rituals. If you live in a place where you feel safe to work outdoors, by all means do so. Do what feels comfortable for you—the choice is yours. Although these ritual suggestions are presented for individual use, they can easily be done with a group.

The focus in *The Goddess Oracle* is on nourishment and finding what is right for you. Let go of any need "to do it right" and listen to what you need to do for yourself. *The Goddess Oracle* is here to support you on your own nourishing path.

2
INVOKING THE ORACLE

There are many ways to weave *The Goddess Oracle* into your own personal web of support. There are as many ways to connect with the Goddesses as there are women.

Follow the spreads (a spread is a way to lay out the cards in front of you) listed in the next chapter, make up your own spreads, or use spreads from other favorite oracle systems. Read the descriptions of the cards in the accompanying book or just use the cards to prompt the Goddesses to speak directly through you. The cards were designed to evoke a particular quality while leaving room for your imagination and intuition.

Find a time when you won't be disturbed. You may choose to burn some incense or light a candle—anything to signify that this isn't ordinary time and space, but magical time and space. Allow yourself to breathe until you feel calm and centered. Then ask the Goddesses for support. You can name your specific situation, for example, "What can I do to become successful?," or you can ask for general support; you can ask for help, or you

INVOKING THE ORACLE

can ask a question. Be sure to ask for what you need in a clear, concise, unambiguous manner.

Shuffle the deck while focusing on your particular need or request. When you feel ready, start choosing the cards and placing them face down. Breathe deeply to center yourself and, when you feel ready, pick a card and turn it over. Take time to really feel the presence of that Goddess before you. Feel that she is filling you with the quality she represents. Then when you feel ready, go on to the next card and the next, until you have turned over all the cards in front of you.

Now turn to the section in the book that describes the Goddesses you've selected and read about them and their meanings in response to yo question. Or simply let the images depicted on the cards speak to you intuitively. You may want to meditate on these images and see what arises in your consciousness.

The simplest way to use *The Goddess Oracle* is to draw a single card. Ask your question and open your heart for the answer while mixing the deck. When you feel ready, pick a card. Here are possible questions for the one-card draw:

- What do I need to know about the current situation I am in?
- How can I nurture wholeness in this situation?
- If I were to do (name a course of action), what would need to be nourished?
- What aspect of myself do I need to nourish to bring about wholeness?

EXAMPLE: Carol wanted to make some changes in the way she was expressing herself artistically, but wasn't sure how to go about it. She asked: "What aspect of myself do I need to nourish in order to enhance my creativity?" The card she chose was **Brigid:** *Inspiration*, which she interpreted to mean that she needed to draw more deeply from her "inner well." She also needed to relax and open up to the flow of creative energy, trusting her intuition rather than relying so much on her intellect. Once she did this, Carol felt inspired to try some new techniques and her artwork became more vivid and exciting.

Another way of using the simplicity and directness of a one-card draw is to ask, "Which Goddess do I need to be nourished by today?" and select a card. Then place the Goddess card before you. As you gaze at her, allow yourself to feel nourished by her. Allow yourself to call her in to walk with you today. Then envision yourself becoming her.

EXAMPLE: Using **Durga:** *Boundaries*, you could feel yourself holding her sword in one hand and sitting on a tiger, ready to do battle with demons. You could feel her power flowing through you, nourishing you and activating the flow of your own power. You could then carry the Goddess card around in your pocket or place her on your altar, your refrigerator, or your computer terminal as a reminder.

When you feel you have received what you needed, thank the Goddesses for their support and return their cards to your deck.

3
THE SPREADS

The Yoni Spread

The *yoni,* or downward pointing triangle, is the symbol of the Feminine. According to Barbara Walker's *Women's Encyclopedia of Myths and Secrets,* "The Yoni Yantra or triangle was known as the Primordial Image, representing the Great Mother as source of all life."

The Yoni Spread nourishes wholeness by focusing your awareness on the three aspects of your Feminine Self: your Wise Woman, your emotional body, and your sexuality. In the millennia of time known as the patriarchy, the Feminine and everything associated with the Feminine has been invalidated. You don't need a divination system to tell you that. Just look at how women's sexuality is feared, how women's emotions are dismissed and ridiculed, how the Wise Woman archetype is represented as an evil witch, her wisdom denigrated as "Old Wives' Tales."

The way to heal the wounding done by the patriarchy is first to acknowledge the wounding, then to ask what you can do to heal that wound. By allowing a wound to tell its story, you bear witness and validate its experience. What heals the hurt is the willingness to listen and then acknowledge the wounding.

The Yoni Spread assists you in healing your Feminine Self by giving each of the three parts of your Feminine Self a voice—the voice of the Goddess. Just pick a card and listen.

1
Nourishing wholeness in your Wise Woman

2
Nourishing wholeness in your emotional body

3
Nourishing wholeness in your sexuality

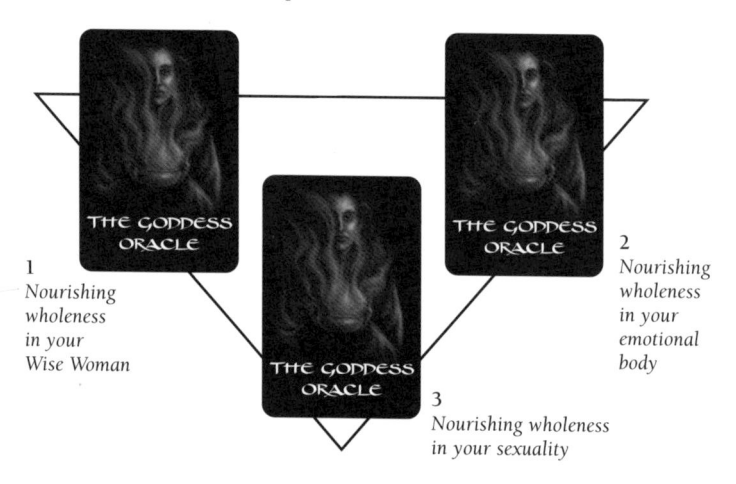

Diagram of Yoni Spread

The first card (upper left point of the triangle) shows how to nourish wholeness in your Wise Woman, the source of your feminine inner knowing and wisdom. The second card (upper right point of the triangle) represents how to nourish wholeness in your emotional body, how to express your feelings rather than repress them. The third card (downward point of the triangle) indicates what is needed to nourish wholeness in your sexuality, your source of energy, power, and creativity. By combining the energy inherent in your Wise Woman, your emotional body, and your sexuality, the

THE SPREADS

Yoni Spread assists you in coming into right relationship with your Feminine Self.

Some possible requests for the Yoni Spread are:

- How can I nourish wholeness right now?
- What will be the effect on my Feminine Self if I open to (state the person or situation about which you want advice)?

EXAMPLE: Rachel was having excruciating menstrual cramps. She had tried everything: prescription drugs, birth control pills, and dietary changes. I suggested she use *The Goddess Oracle*, the Yoni Spread. Rachel's request was "Advise me on how to nourish wholeness, so my menstrual cramps will stop."

Diagram of Rachel's Yoni Spread

For Wise Woman (the first card, upper left point of triangle) she drew **Amaterasu**: *Beauty*. I asked her how she felt about her Wise

Woman, and Rachel said she felt at war with her. As a child she received strong intuitive flashes about things she needed to do or ways of acting in situations, but her mother always insisted that Rachel do things her mother's way. That usually proved disastrous for her. As an adult, Rachel had no past basis of trusting her Wise Woman, yet she still got strong intuitive flashes. This left her feeling uneasy and conflicted.

The Wise Woman aspect of a young woman is nurtured by being listened to and by being respected. Rachel interpreted **Amaterasu:** *Beauty* to mean she needed to regard her Wise Woman as beautiful, as something to appreciate, rather than to fight.

In the emotional body spot, **Durga:** *Boundaries* revealed herself. "Oh," Rachel gasped when she saw the card, "I don't have boundaries. I tend to feel overwhelmed by my emotional reaction to life, so much so that feeling my emotions can be painful or confusing to me." I suggested that when she learns to honor her emotions and finds a safe way to express them by creating strong boundaries, she won't feel overwhelmed by them.

Demeter: *Feelings/Emotions* was chosen for the point, sexuality. "It figures. I am not in touch with my sexual needs, my sexual feelings. I deny that I have any," Rachel stated. "I see that this is something I will need to get in touch with and work on in order to be healed."

The Place of Opposites Spread

In the eye of the storm there is calmness and peace, and in that place of calmness and peace there is room for vision. In the Place of Opposites, between the dynamic pull of known opposing

THE SPREADS

forces, you can come to clarity. Understanding the forces at work in a particular situation helps you to navigate the best path for yourself.

The Place of Opposites Spread uses four cards. **First card—**What is the light of the situation, or what aspect needs to be focused on? **Second card—**What is the shadow of the situation, or what is hidden that is creating the current situation? **Third card—**What is the action of the situation, or what can be actively done? **Fourth card—**What is the beingness of the situation, or what needs to be experienced?

The Place of Opposites Spread

EXAMPLE: I was in a difficult place. Three days a week I worked at two different jobs. The rest of the time was spent seeing private clients, doing workshops, being my own publicity agent, conducting my shamanic-priestess apprenticeship, and trying to have a social life! In addition, I wanted to write the books I was envisioning. I asked *The Goddess Oracle,* "How can I nurture wholeness in this current situation?" Here is the spread I drew.

Coatlicue: *Grief* appeared as the first card—what is the light of the situation or what aspect needs to be focused on.

The second card was **Nu Kwa**: *Order,* for what is the shadow of the situation or what is hidden that is creating the situation.

Gyhldeptis: *Synthesis* was called into the circle to show what is the action of the situation or what can be done.

Pele: *Awakening* erupted into my spread for what is the beingness of the situation or what needs to be experienced.

I interpreted that the Goddesses were telling me to grieve the loss of time for myself, which is what wanting to write always brings up for me. So I drummed my grief. Then, order was creating this situation. I tend to structure my time very tightly so that I will accomplish everything. My writing time is usually relegated to weekends when I am not giving workshops. When friends invite me to do interesting things, however, I rebel at the way I have ordered my life.

Perhaps, instead of structuring my writing time, I needed another approach. I could seek to synthesize the various areas of my life and find the common thread, so that I wouldn't dissipate my energy. Perhaps I needed to let go of some things I was doing to make more time for myself. Lastly, I needed to awaken my energy and view my writing as nourishing and recharging, rather than as depleting me or keeping me from having fun.

The Goddess Support Group Spread

A "support group" is a group that listens respectfully and offers advice only if asked. When using *The Goddess Oracle* you will be listened to respectfully and you will get advice only if you choose to read it in the book or receive it intuitively.

Shuffle the deck while focusing on your particular need or request. Ask the Goddesses for their support. Name your specific situation, for example, "Give me support at this time in my relationship with X," or ask for general support.

When you feel ready, start choosing Goddess cards—as many as you feel you need to support you. You may need only one Goddess. You may need twelve. It is up to you. Arrange the cards in a circle around you, face down. When you feel ready, choose a card and turn it over. Take as much time as you want to feel the presence of that Goddess before turning over the next card. Feel yourself in a circle surrounded by the Goddesses you have chosen. Let your Goddess Support Group nourish you. Listen to what they have to say to you.

When you feel you have received what you needed, thank the Goddesses for their support and release them from your circle. Put their cards back into your deck.

THE GODDESS ORACLE

The Goddess Oracle can also be used in conjunction with your favorite divination system (*I Ching,* Runes, Tarot, *Voyager Tarot, Medicine Cards,* et cetera). After doing your spread or your throw, ask *The Goddess Oracle,* "How can I use the reading I have just received to nurture wholeness in my life?" *The Goddess Oracle* will offer you additional insights and expand the spectrum of the guidance you've received from your other divination method.

PART TWO

THE GODDESSES

AMATERASU OMI KAMI
BEAUTY

Let me share with you the secret of the mirror
let me share what is known only to the Sun Goddess
It is a secret so powerful
it will free you from darkness
a secret so delightful
it lets warmth dance in your heart
a secret so illuminating
it allows you to know yourself
a secret so simple
all you need do is open your eyes
the secret is
in the light of the sun
in the eyes of the mirror
you are Beauty

Mythology

Amaterasu (pronounced *a-ma-te-ra-tsoo*) **Omi Kami** is the Shinto Sun Goddess of Japan. When insulted by her crude brother, Susano-o, the Storm God, she withdrew into a cave and refused to come out. Distressed by the withdrawal of the sun, **Uzume**, the Shaman-Goddess, did a comical bawdy dance to entertain the Gods and Goddesses and to provoke **Amaterasu**'s curiosity. When **Amaterasu** opened her door to peek, she was dazzled by her own beauty, reflected to her in a mirror the Gods and Goddesses had installed, and came out.

Meaning of the Card

Amaterasu is here to tell you to bask in the radiance of your own beauty. Do you know your unique beauty or do you feel you can't be beautiful because you don't look like a model or movie star? Are you in your crone years and feel that age is ugly? Perhaps you are afraid to express your beauty, afraid that you will attract unwanted energies. (If so, you may also want to work with **Durga**: *Boundaries,* pp. 56–59.) **Amaterasu** says that all women possess the light of the Feminine and that light is beauty. She advises you to let go of your preconceptions about what beauty is and allow your beauty to be. Wholeness is nurtured when we celebrate all our aspects and being female means that we are beautiful.

Ritual Suggestion: Beauty Bath

All you need for this ritual is a mirror and the willingness to see your beauty.

Find a time and place when and where you will not be disturbed. Sit or lie comfortably with your spine straight. You may remove your clothes or do the ritual with your clothes on, whichever is appropriate for you. When you feel ready, take a deep breath and release it letting everything go. Then take four more deep breaths, focusing on the rhythm of your breathing. If at any time during this ritual you feel uncomfortable or are afraid of doing anything suggested, just take a deep breath, experience the feelings while continuing to breathe deeply, then slow down and continue at your own pace.

When you feel relaxed and ready, pick up the mirror. Look at your face. Just look. If judgments or criticisms come up, acknowledge them, then let them go. Focus on the uniqueness that is you, reflected in your face. Look at your face and allow yourself to feel compassion, tenderness, acceptance, and love.

Next look at your eyes. Say to yourself: "My eyes are beautiful." Look at your nose and tell yourself: "My nose is beautiful." Then your forehead, cheeks, mouth/lips, teeth, ears, skin, bone structure. When you are finished enjoying the beauty of your face, go on to the rest of your body. When you have acknowledged your entire body, take a deep breath and look in the mirror. Tell yourself: "I (name) am beautiful." Say it over and over. Allow yourself to bathe in your appreciation of your own beauty, till you feel a tingle of appreciation and delight. Continue for as long as you wish, till you are filled with your beauty.

When you feel ready, take a deep breath and exhale to the sound of "ahhhh." Take another deep breath and bring your attention back to this time and place. Welcome back!

APHRODITE

LOVE

When I open my heart
I am filled
with delight so profound
with ecstasy so sweet
with pleasure so deep
the connecting with my beloved
takes me to all the places
and the union

plays rhapsodies in my soul
I can achieve union
when I achieve oneness
with myself
I can dance partnership
when I can dance alone
I can love another
when I can love myself

Mythology

Aphrodite (pronounced *a-fro-dye'tee*), ancient Mediterranean Mother Goddess, traveled to Greece when the Greeks colonized Canaan. The Greeks say **Aphrodite** was born of the union of the sky and the fertile sea womb, when the castrated penis of the former Sky God Uranus fell into the ocean. Although traditionally revered in all her multitudinous aspects, including battle, the Greeks, in their effort to assimilate her, relegated her to a love Goddess. When she arrived at Olympus, Zeus, the chief God, married her to Hephaestus, the lame God of smithcraft. He made her exquisite jewelry, but she preferred the passionate Ares, God of war, in her bed.

Meaning of the Card

Aphrodite is here with her dance of love, inviting you to luxuriate, bask, and revel in love for yourself. Do you spend the day without thinking or saying how much you love yourself? Do you do little loving things for yourself? Or are you miserly, keeping yourself on a diet of starvation rations? Do you listen to your needs in a loving, respectful way, or do you criticize yourself for balking at the schedule you keep, for complaining about the job you hate, for bemoaning the relationship you endure? Now is the time to love yourself. **Aphrodite** says that to be able to love another, you must be able to love yourself. Loving others means being able to allow them to be exactly as they are. It means witnessing yourself and your loved ones with love, amusement, and delight. The amount of space we can allow another is dependent on the amount of space we can allow for ourselves. Wholeness is achieved when we can hold infinite space and patience for ourselves first and then extend it to others.

Ritual Suggestion: Holding Space

This can be done anytime, anywhere, for as long as you feel is appropriate. Take a deep breath and release it. Take another deep breath and as you release it feel, sense, or see a circle of space around you. It can be any amount of space that you need. Now fill that space with love in any form that pleases, delights, tickles, or makes you feel good. Once the circle is filled, put yourself in the center of the circle, in the middle of all that love, and take it into your cells, into the marrow of your bones. Take it in, whether or not you feel you deserve it. Take it in, regardless of how you feel about yourself. See, sense, or feel yourself filling with love for you. As you are holding the space for you, look into your own eyes and say: "I love you." Keep repeating it over and over until you feel your love for yourself dancing in your heart. Feel the love circulate through your body. Now take a deep breath, exhale slowly, and open your eyes. Welcome back!

ARTEMIS

SELFHOOD

I am who I am
and I know who I am
I can take care of myself
under all circumstances
and I can let others care for me
I can choose
There is no authority
higher than my own
my powers of discernment are finely honed
I am autonomous
I am free from the influence
of others' opinions
I am able to separate
that which needs separation
so a clear decision
can be reached
I think for myself
I set my sights
and aim my bow
my arrows always find their mark

Mythology

Artemis (pronounced *ar'teh-mis*), another multidimensional Goddess reduced by the Greeks to the domain of moon, virgin, huntress, and childbirth, really represented the Feminine in all her aspects. She was the huntress who protected animals and the virgin (whole and complete unto herself) who made love in the woods. When **Artemis** was a little girl, Zeus, her father, wanted to give her a gift and asked her what she wanted. **Artemis** replied: I want to run forever wild and free with my hounds in the woods and never, ever marry.

Meaning of the Card

Artemis has shot her arrow of selfhood into your life to help you focus on yourself. Have you been too much at the service of others without making sure you get what you need for yourself? Has it been too long since you had time to yourself or a space of your own? Do the boundaries of your selfhood seem blurred and indistinct? Do you feel you have no right to a self of your own, but must always be thinking of others, putting their needs first, until you don't know who you are or what you want? Now is the time to come into yourself. Now is the time to pay attention to the whispering voices of your own needs. Now is the time to take yourself back and celebrate and strengthen who you are. **Artemis** says that wholeness is nurtured when you honor, respect, and give time to yourself. She also asks how can you expect to hit any targets if you don't have a self from which to shoot?

Ritual Suggestion: Taking Yourself Back

This can be done at any time and in any place. You may choose to do it alone or in front of the person or people to whom you have given pieces of yourself.

Sit, stand, or lie with your spine straight. Close your eyes. Take a deep breath and release it. Take another deep breath, breathing into your womb, your center. Look at your body. Ask yourself if there are any missing pieces. Open to allow yourself to get a sense, image, or feeling of where those missing pieces are. For example: Did you give your lover your joy piece and now can't experience joy without him/her? Did you give your children a large chunk of yourself and now that they're grown you feel lost? Call those pieces home. Sense, feel, or see those missing pieces coming back to you. Let them reenter your body and, as they do, feel yourself grow stronger and more vital. When you are finished taking yourself back, you may want to reinforce your boundaries and name your pieces. (See **Durga:** *Boundaries,* pp. 56–59.) Thank your pieces for returning, and open your eyes. Welcome back!

BABA YAGA

WILD WOMAN

I walk in the forest
and speak intimately with the animals
I dance barefoot in the rain
without any clothes
I travel on pathways
that I make myself
and in ways that suit me
my instincts are alive and razor sharp
my intuition and sense of smell are keen
I freely express my vitality
my sheer exuberant joyfulness
to please myself

THE GODDESSES

because it is natural
it is what needs to be
I am the wild joyous life force
Come and meet me

Mythology

Baba Yaga (pronounced *bah-bye'yegg-ah*), Slavic birth-death wild Goddess, rode about in a mortar—an extremely hard bowl used with a pestle to grind grain, nuts, et cetera. Her ways were fierce and wild, deep and penetrating, and could be interpreted as grinding away that which was extraneous. **Baba Yaga**'s house stood on chicken legs and danced about. Her time of death was autumn, for she was the life force present in the harvested grain. In Russia this Goddess was transformed into a witch who lived deep in the forest and ate children.

Meaning of the Card

Baba Yaga flies into your life in her mortar to help you nurture wholeness by getting in touch with your wild woman. It is time to reconnect with the natural, the primal, the instinctual. It is time to shake out your hair, your body, and shake up your life. Have you banished your wild woman to the dungeon? Have you chained her, muzzled her, caged her, lest people find out you are not nice, neat, and clean? Free her! You need her. That wild woman is part of your joy, part of your vitality, part of your creativity. She is you and you need every part of yourself in order to dance wholeness. **Baba Yaga** says it is most important for you to learn to integrate your wild woman because an unintegrated wild woman creates self-destructive behavior. The wildness is there and needs to be expressed. It is your choice whether to express it creatively or destructively.

Ritual Suggestion: Retrieving Your Wild Woman

Find a time and a place when and where you will not be disturbed. Sit or lie comfortably with your spine straight and close your eyes. Take a deep breath and release it with a sound. Take another deep breath and release it with a hum. See, sense, or feel the image of a tree. It can be any tree, one you have seen before or one that exists in your imagination. Take a third deep breath and, as you release it, stand before that tree. Walk around the tree. On the other side of the tree you see a huge opening in the trunk. Step into that opening. Once inside the tree, feel yourself sinking. Down, down, down you go, traveling inside the root of the tree. It feels safe and comfortable and you surrender to the sensation of floating down, down, down. As you reach the end of the root, you find yourself on a slide that takes you right into the Underworld, where you land on a soft cushion.

It is time to call your wild woman. You can whistle or howl, chant or sing, dance or play music to call her. When your wild woman arrives, thank her for showing up. Ask her for what you need. You may not know what you need, but she will and she will give it to you. In return, she'll ask you for a gift. Give her what she asks for with an open heart. Now ask her if she is willing to come back with you and be part of your life. She says yes and you hug her, and as you do, you feel yourself and the wild woman merging, becoming one. You feel a sense of being augmented, strengthened, expanded. You feel a surge of vitality and joy.

THE GODDESSES

Now it is time to come back. Return to the tree root. Sense yourself floating up, up, up, feeling refreshed, energized, renewed, revitalized. Up, up, up until you reach the inside of the trunk of the tree. You step out and take a deep breath, and as you release it return to your body. When you feel ready, open your eyes. Welcome back!

BAST

PLAY

I swirl and twirl
I hide and seek
romping and ranging
funning and frolicking
my opportunities
for self-amusement are endless
and the pleasure
that it gives me
makes me purr
Life's challenges never stop me
for I know how to whole myself
with play

Mythology

In Egypt, **Bast** (pronounced *bahst*), the cat-headed Goddess, and **Sekhmet**, the lion-headed Goddess, represented two powerful aspects of the sun: the life-giving, pleasurable aspect and the burning, destroying aspect. **Bast** was worshipped at Bubastis, where vast celebrations were held. She ruled pleasure, joy, music, dance, health and healing, the moon, and of course, cats.

Meaning of the Card

Bast bats at you with her paw to urge you to come and play with her. It is time to divert yourself with something that is amusing, fun, and totally recreational. Has play been a low priority for you? Do you know how to play? What does play mean to you? Perhaps you've been working so hard that you've forgotten to give yourself a play break. **Bast** tells you the way to nurture wholeness lies in engaging in play. It is time to discover the ways you are able to play and do it!

Ritual Suggestion: Playtime with Bast

Find a time and a place where and when you will not be disturbed. Sit or lie comfortably with your spine straight and close your eyes. Take a deep breath and release it slowly. Take another deep breath and inhale large gulps of rose-colored contentment. As you exhale, let the contentment spread throughout your body.

Take a deep breath and, as you release it, see, sense, or feel a large hole in the ground. Take another deep breath and, as you release it, stand outside the hole. It is large enough for you to enter and, as you do, you find yourself in an underground tunnel. The tunnel is well lit, warm, and comfortable. Allow yourself to go down, down, down, deeper and deeper and deeper. Down, down, down, feeling more and more relaxed, until you see a light at the end of the tunnel. That is the Underworld. You step out into the

THE GODDESSES

Underworld and call on **Bast**. She appears in her cat form beside you and asks you what you need. You tell her you are here to play with her. She lets out an excited meow and asks you to climb up on her back. You do and off you go flying through the air. As you peer down, you see the ocean and the shore. **Bast** lands gently on a beautiful white sand beach and invites you to build sandcastles with her. You accept and she transforms herself into an appropriately aged playmate for you. She says you can play here alone with her or invite others. Do what is right for you. You can invite people you know, people you don't know, imaginary people, or play alone with her.

On the beach is a large box of shovels and pails. You and **Bast** decide what you want the castle to look like, then you both begin. After some time has passed, you both feel hot and decide to go for a swim. You run into the water, which is very comfortable. **Bast** splashes you and you splash her. Then **Bast** invites you to play a game of shape-shifting in which you chase each other while changing shapes. At first you both shape-shift into dolphins and you frolic in the sea. Then you change into seagulls and play tag in the air. Keep changing shapes until you are ready to stop, then change back into yourself and walk out of the sea.

It is now time for you to return. **Bast** transforms herself back into a cat and you climb onto her back. Up you both go till you are back in the Underworld, next to the tunnel. You thank **Bast** and enter the tunnel.

Now you are traveling up, up, up, feeling light and refreshed; up, up, up, feeling relaxed and rejuvenated, ready for anything; up, up, up, till you are back at the hole in the ground. You step out and take a deep breath. As you slowly release it, you come back into your body. You take another deep breath and open your eyes. Welcome back!

BLODEUWEDD

BETRAYAL

Created out of flowers
and made for pleasure
I was given to Llew Llaw Gyffes as wife
We were happy
and spent many hours
making love
till he left
one morning for the High King's court
That day another man came along
and it was he I wanted
His caresses were sweeter
his manhood was stronger
he promised not to leave me . . .
I could not live without him
Together we plotted the death of my husband
and carried it out one year hence
We thought we killed Llew
but he returned a year later and
killed my lover

THE GODDESSES

I ran, to get away, hoping to escape
but the pounding hooves of my pursuers
caught up with me
The magician who turned me from flowers
into a woman
turned me from a woman into an owl
as punishment for my betrayal

Mythology

Welsh earth Goddess **Blodeuwedd** (pronounced *blow-dye'wed*) was wedded to sun God Llew Llaw Gyffes (Lugh) on the Midsummer holiday of Lughnassah. Her name has become associated with betrayal because she tricked her husband by getting him to enact the complicated means of his death: bathing under a thatched roof over a cauldron by the side of a river, while standing with one leg touching a deer. Then she killed him with the help of her lover. The real story is about the archetypal forces. **Blodeuwedd** represents the voracious earth Goddess hungry for the blood of the sacred king to fertilize her soil.

Meaning of the Card

Blodeuwedd's hooting call is heard in your life, alerting you to a betrayal. How is betrayal showing up in your life? Do you have trouble picking trustworthy friends, partners, coworkers, mates? Does all your care, consideration, and loyalty meet with treachery and betrayal? Have you misled someone so that you could get what you wanted? **Blodeuwedd** says that on your path to wholeness you must answer the question "How have I betrayed myself?" for all betrayal stems from self-betrayal.

Ritual Suggestion: Journey to Blodeuwedd

Find a time and a place when and where you will not be disturbed. Sit or lie comfortably with your spine straight and close your eyes. Take a deep breath, breathing in safety as you speak or think the words: "I am in a safe space." Take another deep breath and breathe in protection with the words: "I am protected." Take a third deep breath, breathing in acceptance with the words: "I am accepted." Notice if any feelings come up when you breathe in safety, protection, and acceptance.

Now see, feel, or sense a place in nature where you can go to relax. It can be a place you know and visit regularly or one that exists only in your imagination. Take a deep breath and as you exhale, go there. What are the smells? the colors or textures? Take another deep breath and, as you release it, settle in and let go.

When you feel ready, call **Blodeuwedd**. She appears before you and asks you what you need. You ask her for help in healing the root of your self-betrayal and she agrees to help you. **Blodeuwedd** produces a movie screen several feet in front of you. With a snap of her fingers, she begins to run a film. The film is your childhood from the moment of your birth in this life. She asks you to hold the question "When in my childhood was I betrayed?" in your heart. The "film" reaches the originating moment of your betrayal and stops. If any feelings come up, allow yourself to feel them.

THE GODDESSES

Do what is appropriate for you. Were you abandoned? Was someone you trusted not there for you? Were your childhood needs not met? Whatever it is, allow yourself to see what happened. Allow the wounded child that is in you to express the emotion accompanying that betrayal.

Blodeuwedd asks you to go up to the screen, take the hand of that child, and escort her off the screen. You return with her to where you were sitting or lying. Ask that child what she needs and give it to her. Now tell her that you, the adult, love her and won't betray her. Tell her you really see how she was wounded and that you, the adult, will be there for her. Keep repeating this until you feel she has really heard you. Now take her back to the "film" and let her reenter. **Blodeuwedd** rolls back the scene of your originating betrayal and replays it. This time when the betrayal is about to happen, you the adult appear on the scene and protect you the child.

Take in the healing that has occurred. Breathe it deeply into your cells, your bones, your consciousness. You feel energized and calm. You thank **Blodeuwedd** and she asks you for a gift. You give it to her with an open heart, and she disappears.

Now focus your attention on being in your relaxing place in nature. Take a deep breath and, as you release it, touch your left earlobe. Take another deep breath and, as you release it, squeeze your eyelids. Take one last deep breath and open your eyes. Welcome back!

BRIGID

INSPIRATION

Let me come to you
through the mists
through the fire
through the plants
through the deep flowing wells
with ideas
visions
words
music beyond the tips of your ears
Let me move you
enliven you
stimulate you
till your perspective shifts
and your mind/body/spirit explodes
and you are left standing
in the wake of what has been revealed . . .
and life feels very sweet

Mythology

Brigid (pronounced *bridge'id*), which means "bright," is a Celtic triple Goddess of fire: the fire of inspiration, smithcraft, poetry, healing, and divination. Her inspiration was vital to the bards (poets) who called upon her freely. Legend says that **Brigid** was born with a flame reaching out from the top of her head, connecting her with the universe. The new (Christian) and the old (pagan) **Brigid** were merged into St. Brigid in A.D. 450. St. Brigid, daughter of a druid, was a goldsmith and healer. Nineteen priestesses/nuns guard her sacred fire in Kildare, Ireland. On the twentieth of each month it is said she appears and tends it herself.

Meaning of the Card

Brigid comes to ignite you with inspiration. Are you feeling a lack of direction? motivation? energy? Has your path gone out of focus, your life become unclear? Are you yearning for something but can't quite put your finger on it? It is time to nurture wholeness by taking in the sparkle and crackle of inspiration. **Brigid** says that a life without the fire of inspiration is dull indeed. She further counsels that by allowing inspiration to nurture your life you become sharper, clearer, and more energetic.

Ritual Suggestion: Journey to Brigid

Find a time and place when and where you will not be disturbed. Sit or lie comfortably with your spine straight and close your eyes. When you feel ready, take a deep breath and release it with a sigh, letting go of all you need to let go of. Take another deep breath and let it go with a hiss. Take a third deep breath and, as you release it, picture or sense a cave, a cave you have visited before or one that exists only in your mind. Now take another deep breath and, as you release it, stand before the cave. Run your fingers along the wall of the cave. Smell the cave. Enter it.

Inside, the cave is well lit and warm, and you find yourself going down, down, down, deeper and deeper and deeper. It is a pleasant and comfortable feeling to go down, down, down, deeper and deeper and deeper. There is a light at the end of the cave. You are at the threshold, the place where the cave ends and the Otherworld begins. Step out now into the Otherworld. Notice the dazzling sunlight, the freshness in the air, the vivid colors.

Brigid is waiting for you beside an ancient stone well. You walk over to her across the soft, spongy, emerald grass. She tells you she is happy to see you and glad that you have arrived. You tell her you seek inspiration. **Brigid** asks you for a gift and you give it to her gladly. Then she rings you in a circle of fire and lights a fire in your crown chakra (top of your head). You feel a tingling and stimulating of that point. You feel your energy opening and expanding. Your power to visualize clears and grows stronger. You feel inspired!

It is time for you to say good-bye. You thank **Brigid**. She tells you all you need to do to activate inspiration is to visualize that flame at the top of your head. You enter the cave. Now you are coming up, up, up, through the warm comfort of the cave, feeling relaxed, energized, refreshed. Up, up, up, till you reach the entrance of the cave. Move outside the cave, take a deep breath, and as you slowly exhale you are back in your body. Take another deep breath and when you exhale, if ready, open your eyes. Welcome back!

CERRIDWEN

DEATH AND REBIRTH

I give you life
I give you death
it is all one

You travel the spiral path
the eternal path
that is existence
ever becoming
ever growing
ever changing
Nothing dies that is not reborn
nothing is born that does not die
When you come to me
I welcome you home
then I take you into my womb
my cauldron of transformation
where you are stirred and sifted
blended and boiled
melted and mashed
reconstituted then recycled
You always come back to me
you always go forth renewed
Death and Rebirth are but points of transition
along the Eternal Path

Mythology

To the Welsh, **Cerridwen** (pronounced *ker'rid-when*) is a triple Goddess—Maid, Mother, and Crone—whose totem animal is the great white sow. She is associated with the moon, inspiration, poetry, prophecy, shape-shifting, and life and death. **Cerridwen** had two boys. One was beautiful and one was ugly. Because she wanted the ugly one to have something of his own, she made him a magical brew. The brew took a year and a day to complete and would make him inspired and brilliant. She set Gwion, her assistant, to watch the brew and bade him not to drink it. Accidentally, some drops of the brew splashed onto his hand and he put his hand in his mouth. Instantly he knew everything, including the fact that **Cerridwen** would seek his death. He ran away and she ran after him. After many shape-shiftings, he was swallowed by **Cerridwen** who gave birth to him nine months later.

Meaning of the Card

Cerridwen's appearance in your life heralds a time of death and rebirth. Something is dying and needs to be let go of, so something new can be born. We know the earth's dance of death and rebirth as the seasons. Matter cannot be created or destroyed, but undergoes transformation. So do we. To live fully and in wholeness we need to accept life in all that it is, which includes death and rebirth. Let go of what does not serve you and your wholeness.

Perhaps you have reached the end of a cycle, a relationship, a job, and you fear letting it go. Or feel that you are dying, when only a piece of you needs to give way to the new. Perhaps the idea that there is death and only death is too painful for you to accept. Living in a patriarchal culture has deprived most of us of the Goddess's way of death and rebirth. Wholeness is nurtured when we become conscious that every step on the path of life is also a step toward death and rebirth. Wholeness is achieved when we can say yes and do our dance with death and rebirth. **Cerridwen** says you will always get back what you give to me. It will be changed, it will be transformed, but you will get it back.

THE GODDESSES

Ritual Suggestion: Cerridwen's Cauldron

Find a time and a place when and where you will not be disturbed. Sit or lie comfortably with your spine straight. Close your eyes. Take a deep breath and release it slowly to a count of ten. Take another deep breath and release it again to a count of ten. Take a third deep breath and, as you release it, see, feel, or sense a tunnel. It can be a tunnel you know or one you imagine. Stand outside of the tunnel and run your fingers along the entryway. Smell it. Enter the tunnel. It is warm and comfortable, well lit and pleasant, and you go down, down, down, deeper and deeper and deeper. Down, down, down, feeling relaxed, comfortable, until you reach the end of the tunnel. There is light at the end of the tunnel, the light of the Otherworld.

You step out into the Otherworld and are met by **Cerridwen**. She takes your hand and leads you to her cauldron. It is enormous and black. **Cerridwen** stirs the cauldron. She asks you to put in the cauldron whatever needs to be transformed or let go of, whatever needs to die. You put it in the cauldron and watch. **Cerridwen** stirs the cauldron.

Cerridwen finishes stirring, puts down her staff, and reaches into the cauldron. She takes out what you put in and places it in front of you. It has been transformed into exactly what it needs to be. You thank **Cerridwen** and she asks you for a gift; you give it to her freely. Ready to return, you walk back to the tunnel, taking with you what has been transformed in **Cerridwen**'s cauldron.

Now you are going up, up, up, feeling refreshed, energized. Up, up, up, until you are back at the entrance of the tunnel. You walk out of the tunnel and take a deep breath. As you release it slowly, you come back into your body. Take another deep breath and, if ready, open your eyes. Welcome back!

CHANGING WOMAN

CYCLES

I am what comes round again and again
what can never die
I renew myself in the seasons
in the cycle of time
the great round
I bleed yet do not die
I keep my blood within and become wise
I dance the spiral
and keep changing

Mythology

Changing Woman, or Estsanatlehi (self-renewing one)—as she is called by the Navajo and Apache—can change her age merely by walking into the horizon. White Shell Woman and Turquoise Woman are among her many names, which correspond to the changing colors of her dress as the seasons change. The Navajo say that she was found by Coyote, after being born of Darkness and Dawn on Spruce Mountain, with a blanket of clouds and rainbows, secured in her cradleboard by lightning and sunbeams. Her gifts to the people are the Blessingway ceremonies, the seasons, and food.

THE GODDESSES

Meaning of the Card

Changing Woman comes spinning into your life to tell you the way to wholeness for you lies in learning to honor your cycles. Menstrual cycles are an important aspect of being female. We bleed but do not die, and therefore can bring forth life. As we continue to dance our cycles, we reach the time of menopause when we leave our childbearing years behind and hold our wise blood within. We can then be a resource for our loved ones and community by becoming hags, which means "women of wisdom."

Do you celebrate your menstruation and view it as a time for you to go within? as a time to let go, let die, so the new can come? Or have you bought into the patriarchal view that it is a curse, something unclean, something to be hidden away? Does menopause automatically fill you with fear of becoming old and ugly, no longer valuable and worthy in a culture that adores youth? Do you feel invalidated in a society that urges women to hide their bleeding times, regulate their hormones by taking pills, and postpone menopause through ERT (estrogen replacement therapy)?

Honoring your cycles also means honoring your own unique process, your own unique path in life. You may be in the midst of a particular life cycle that you need to surrender to and honor. **Changing Woman** says that wholeness is nurtured when we reclaim the power of our cycles by paying attention to them and celebrating them. By celebrating our cycles, we celebrate ourselves as women.

Ritual Suggestion: Celebrating Your Cycles

Find a time and a place where and when you will not be disturbed. Sit, stand, or lie comfortably and identify the cycle you are in. You may choose to find or make a symbol of your present cycle. Cast a circle by calling in (speaking to the elements and asking them to be present) or by becoming the elements (see **Vila:** *Shape-shifting,* pp. 174–177). If you are using a symbol, place that symbol in the center of your circle. Walk around the outside of your circle and fill the inside of the circle with respect and honoring. You could fill it by putting on your favorite dance music and dancing around the circle, thinking or chanting "I love my cycles, I love being a woman." You could drum or play a musical instrument. You can do anything that celebrates you and your cycles. Be sure to notice if any feelings come up and allow yourself to express them.

Continue until you feel the energy in the circle is strong, then step in and breathe it deep into your cells. Lie, sit, or stand in the circle, whatever is comfortable for you. Let the celebratory energy you have built up nourish you to the very core of your body/mind/spirit. Feel its healing power reweave the torn, wounded places inside. Feel yourself as a woman, proud to be a woman, proud to bleed, proud to hold your wise blood within, proud to be in the midst of whatever cycle you are in. When you feel full, give thanks to **Changing Woman**, to yourself, to your womanhood. Step out of the circle. Release what you have called in. Welcome back!

COATLICUE

GRIEF

With my head heavy with loss
with my eyes blinded by tears
I wander
unable to rest
unable to find ease
I am dry
my bones
are dust in the desert sun
my heart
ripped out
lies broken on the ground
each step I take in living
tramples it anew
each breath I take in living
ruptures my wounds
how can I bear the unbearable
how can I survive the insurmountable
will my sorrow ever end?
will my loss ever be filled?
will my longing ever cease?

Mythology

Coatlicue (pronounced *co-at'le-kew*), or Serpent Skirt, is mother of the Aztec deities. She gets her name because she wears a skirt made of swinging rattlesnakes. She is worshipped as earth mother and life-and-death mother. She found some white-plumed feathers one day and, placing them on her breast, became pregnant. When the other Gods, her children, discovered her pregnancy, they swore to kill her to keep her new offspring from supplanting them. Only her beloved daughter, Coyolxauhqul, the Moon Goddess, warned her mother. Coyolxauhqul was decapitated by the Sun God and the grieving **Coatlicue** placed her daughter's luminous head in the sky.

Meaning of the Card

Coatlicue is here to help bring you face-to-face with your grief. She is here to tell you that there is no way around grief, there is no place you can hide from grief. The way to wholeness lies in going through your grief. Have you been afraid to face the pain that accepting grief and going through the grief process will bring? Have you been hiding from grief, pretending you are really okay? Perhaps you fear the grief is so great that you will remain in it for the rest of your life. Have you done some of your grieving, but not all of it, so that it catches you unaware in odd moments? Perhaps you are staying in a situation you need to leave, but fear the grief that leaving would engender. It is imperative for your healing process that you grieve. It is time to wail and keen and moan. It is time to ask for support from friends and family. Life is about loss and loss is part of life. The seasons change and all is in a state of transition. Even grief, if fully faced, will finally lessen. In time you will feel stronger and more alive. One day your wounds will fade to scars. Remember that your process takes as long as it needs to take and that everyone's time of grief is different. **Coatlicue** tells you to feel the grief so the healing can come.

Ritual Suggestion: Drumming Your Grief

You will need a drum with a beater.* Do not use your hands, as you could hurt them or, to protect them, not go fully into the emotion.

Find a time and place when and where you will not be disturbed. Sit comfortably with your spine straight. Take a deep breath and release it. Let everything go. Take a deep breath into your womb, the center of your body, and release it. When you feel centered and relaxed, give yourself the space and permission to open to your grief. Find the place in your body where you are holding grief. Is it in your heart? in your lungs? in your solar plexus? If you are visual, open yourself to let images come to you. If you are kinesthetic, allow your body to feel the grief.

This can be a recent grief or a past one. A grief that was never acknowledged or a grief that was only glanced at. You may find that once you open to grief, many griefs will come flooding into you. Or you may find it hard to grasp. Let what comes up, come up, without censoring, without judging. Just accept.

Once you begin to experience the grief, you are ready to drum. It is not important how you sound. It is important that you make sounds. Allow your own grief rhythm to be expressed. Allow

---

*Ideally, a Native American drum with a handle to hold in one hand and a beater in the other. The drum needs to be sturdy. I would suggest a deerskin drum or any type of strong skin except goat.

yourself to vocalize. Give yourself permission to move or dance or go crazy with grief. Do whatever you need to do. The more you can involve yourself, the more profound and satisfying the experience will be. Let yourself howl and moan and keen and cry. Perhaps your sounds and rhythm will evolve into a specific song that you can sing whenever you need to grieve. Perhaps it will be different for you each time. Do whatever is appropriate for you.

Keep drumming the grief until it changes to something else. Keep going deeper. Ride the grief until it transforms. If this is not the time to do all your grieving, just get your feet wet in the waters of grief now and do more later. Do what is appropriate for you.

When you have drummed your grief and it has transformed, or when you feel you have done what is appropriate for you, put the drum aside. Take a deep breath and release it slowly, inhaling the energy you have raised. Give thanks and praise your courage. When you feel ready, open your eyes. Welcome back!

CORN WOMAN

NOURISHMENT

I give you my breast
the earth
and suckle you with
corn and grain
plants and animals and fish
all to sustain you
all to feed you

THE GODDESSES

all to nourish you
the great giveaway
my love for you
the food
so you will live
prosper and grow
From my breast
the earth
because I love you

CORN WOMAN
NOURISHMENT

Mythology

Southwestern indigenous aboriginals and pueblo peoples—the Arikara, Pawnee, Cheyenne, Mandan, Hidasta, Abnaki, Cherokee, and Huron—see corn as a Goddess. **Corn Woman** encompasses the figures of Corn Mother, the Corn Maidens, and Yellow Woman. They all relate to corn as a sacred being who gives of herself to her people to sustain them and nourish them. The Arikara Creator God, Nesaru, fashioned Corn Mother from an ear of corn which grew in heaven. Corn Mother then came to earth and taught people how to honor the deities and to plant corn.

Meaning of the Card

Corn Woman brings her love for you in the form of food to tell you it is time to nourish yourself. Eating is a sacred act. Something living dies and you take it in, whether you hunt/kill the animals you eat with your own hands or buy your vegetables in the supermarket. Part of being human means causing death in order to live. To treat the act of eating as a chore, as something to be feared or avoided, is to denigrate the gift of love from **Corn Woman** and the plants and the animals.

Do you fear food? Does just looking at food make you feel like you are gaining weight? Are you too busy, too stressed, too involved with more important things than nourishing yourself? Do you nourish others but not yourself? Do you have a love-hate relationship with food? **Corn Woman** says that eating is one of the most basic acts of self-nourishment and that the way to wholeness for you lies in coming into right relationship with food.

Ritual Suggestion: Sacred Eating

The time is breakfast, lunch, or dinner and the place is where you eat your meals. You can do this alone or with loved ones or friends. You can either prepare the food yourself or have others prepare it. When the food is ready, sit at your place. Take a moment to look at the food, to see, sense, or feel the life force of the food before you. Then close your eyes and take a deep breath. Notice if any feelings come up. (You may want to also work with **Demeter:** *Feelings/Emotions,* pp. 53–56.) Now feel the energy from the earth moving up into your toes, into your calves, your thighs, and so on, into each part of your body until you feel centered, focused, aware, and fully in your body. Take another deep breath and feel all your cells breathe with you. Now open your eyes.

Serve yourself some food. Honor the plants and/or animals by saying words of gratitude. As you take a bite, slow down, be with the food, with the sensations, with all your senses. Chew slowly, giving yourself time to really taste, smell, and savor the flavors. Try to taste all the ingredients. With your next bite, focus on the life force. Do you feel a tingling as you chew, like energy surges pulsing in your mouth? Feel how you and the food become one as it dissolves in your mouth. Let yourself take in the life force of the food and feel it nourish your own life force. Give yourself permission to fully enjoy the pleasure you get from eating. Continue to eat in this focused, sacred way, being present in your body, paying attention to all your senses, until you have eaten what you need. When you are finished, take a deep breath and let the energy you have gained circulate throughout your body. Give thanks to **Corn Woman** and to yourself for nourishment.

DEMETER

FEELINGS/EMOTIONS

I felt it all
the rage the anger
the joy the happiness
the tearing the anguish
and I searched
for the middle ground
the sure path
between what I felt
and what I did with it
Then I shed the skins
the layers that build up
when feelings aren't voiced
aren't heard

aren't acknowledged
By giving my feelings
their rightful place
I keep myself far
from the intensity
immensity
sheer density
and cost
of emotion

Mythology

Demeter (pronounced *deh'me-ter*), whose name means "doorway of the mysterious feminine," was worshipped as the Great Goddess long before the patriarchal Greeks conquered the Goddess-worshipping peoples of what is now Greece and imposed their Olympian male-dominated pantheon. As Great Goddess, **Demeter** is known for the founding of agriculture, instituting the social order, and for her mystery rites at Eleusis. One fine spring day, **Demeter**'s daughter Persephone was captured by Hades, god of the Underworld. **Demeter**, in her grief and emotional trauma, withdrew her life force from the earth and winter came. Zeus persuaded Hades to return Persephone to **Demeter**. To trick Persephone into staying with him, for no one could return from the Underworld having eaten the food of the dead, Hades gave Persephone a pomegranate and she ate six seeds. Therefore she was allowed to return to **Demeter** for six months of the year. The other six she spends with Hades in the Underworld.

THE GODDESSES

Meaning of the Card

Demeter has come to light your way through the dark and challenging labyrinth of feelings/emotions. It is time to nurture wholeness by accepting, acknowledging, and expressing your feelings. Feelings are what you feel. Emotions are your reaction to your feelings. Feelings left unexpressed build up and can create disease for they take up space inside and keep healthy energy from flowing.

Perhaps as a child your feelings (and you!) weren't heard, therefore you needed to give them more energy in order to get any sort of a response. Perhaps you fear your emotions and/or feelings will render you too vulnerable, overwhelm you, or take you to places from which you won't be able to return. **Demeter** says the more you learn to accept and acknowledge your feelings, the less time you will spend in emotional turmoil and the more energy you will have to live life. The more you learn to accept and honor your feelings, the safer it will become to express them.

Ritual Suggestion: Saying What Is So

Find a time and a place that is appropriate for you. "Saying What Is So" can be done alone in privacy, in the aftermath of an incident(s) that gave rise to the feelings/emotions, or right in the moment.

Take a deep breath and connect with yourself. Breathe into all the cells of your body. Inhale and exhale through your skin. Take the time to feel present and focused in your body. Then open and ask, "What am I feeling?" Listen for an answer. If one doesn't bubble up, then ask, "Am I angry, happy, sad, joyful, nervous, upset, fearful, et cetera?" Ask your body to speak. If you have a stiff neck, you might ask your neck what it is feeling. State what you feel: "I feel angry," "I feel upset," "I feel hurt," and so on. You may want to say it over and over to yourself. This is the core of "Saying What Is So": getting in touch with the feeling and stating it clearly.

Sometimes our feelings aren't so easy to discern. You may want to relive an incident and unravel the feeling associated with it. Sometimes we have a sense that everything is not right, a sort of unsettledness. Unraveling that sensation and getting to the core feeling helps to dissipate the emotional charge. For example, saying "I feel angry" or "I feel fear" keeps the feeling from escalating into emotion.

DURGA

BOUNDARIES

When threatened by demons
I fiercely protect myself
with all that I am
with all that I have
from deep within
I call forth all that I need
I am the "Inaccessible"
for I place myself beyond the reach of all that would destroy me
all that would annihilate me
all that tries to wound me

THE GODDESSES

I am the "Unapproachable"
for nothing can get at me that I do not willingly let in
I dance my dance of oneness
only with what supports me
nurtures me
loves me
For all that does not
I say: approach at your own risk!

Mythology

Devi is what the Goddess is called in India. To the Hindu, all Goddesses are one goddess, different aspects of Devi or the Divine Feminine. An aspect of Devi was called into being to rid the world of the evil demon **Durga** (pronounced *der'gah*). In the battle between the Gods and the anti-gods or demons, none of the Gods could destroy **Durga**, so they went to Devi and asked for help. Mounting a tiger and brandishing her fearsome weapons, she attacked the demon, who changed from one terrifying form into another until Devi slew him when he transformed into a buffalo. In remembrance of the great battle, Devi took the name of **Durga**.

Meaning of the Card

You have called **Durga** into your life to help you create boundaries.* What are you taking inside that should remain outside? How are you not protecting yourself, your life, your time? Is the

---

* I define boundary as a shield or skin surrounding you that allows you to choose what you take in. All life happens outside of your boundary; you witness it and decide what you are going to take in to nurture yourself.

statement "No, I can't do this right now, I need to care for myself," part of your vocabulary? Perhaps you feel dumped on by others. Are you feeling pulled off center by demands to give and give and give till there is nothing left for yourself? **Durga** is here to assist you in nurturing wholeness by creating and fixing the limits of your personal space. Establishing clear boundaries is an act of self-love. Having no boundaries gives others the message that you are limitless and want to be treated in a limitless way. No one is limitless; there are places where we get hurt, places where we are vulnerable, places that need to be treated with care. **Durga** says that boundaries are vital because they let others know who you are and where you stand.

Ritual Suggestion: Sacred Circle of Self

Find a time and place when and where you will not be disturbed. Sit or lie comfortably with your spine straight and close your eyes. Create a circle around you of any material that makes you feel safe and protected. Once you have created the circle around yourself, make the space within the circle as large or small as you need. It can be miles from the center of the circle to the outer rim or it can be inches. Take as much space as you need.

Now fill your circle with whatever nurtures you. You can fill it with color, flowers, plants, animals—anything you want, so long as it nurtures, supports, and loves you. I strongly urge you not to fill it with people. This is your private space. You are not required to share your space.

The amount of space you need may vary with different situations. Sometimes you may need vast amounts of space and other times, very little. The choice is always yours. The materials you use to create the sacred circle of self may change over time. The sacred circle of self is adaptable and flexible to your needs.

Sit with your sacred circle of self around you until you sense your boundary is in place, ready to protect and nurture you. When ready, open your eyes and come back to the present. To reactivate your sacred circle of self, you need only pause, close your eyes, take a breath, and visualize, sense, or feel it around you.

EOSTRE

GROWTH

I am the movement toward becoming
expanding
enhancing
the impulse deep within all being
to develop
evolve
press onward
to fulfill
all that is possible

Mythology

The Germanic Goddess of fertility, agriculture, and spring, **Eostre** (pronounced *yo'ster*), or **Eastre**, was celebrated with the ritual lighting of dawn fires as a protection for the crops. She symbolizes springtime, new growth, and rebirth. Once, when the

Goddess was late in coming, a little girl found a bird close to death from the cold and turned to **Eostre** for help. A rainbow bridge appeared and **Eostre** came, clothed in her red robe of warm, vibrant sunlight which melted the snows. Spring arrived. Because the little bird was wounded beyond repair, **Eostre** changed it into a snow hare who then brought rainbow eggs. As a sign of spring, **Eostre** instructed the little girl to watch for the snow hare to come to the woods.

Meaning of the Card

Eostre comes into your life with her springtime message of personal growth. It is time to open to things in your life that facilitate growth, development, evolution. Is there a class or workshop you've been wondering if you should take? Do it now! Is there something new that you want to include in your life? Let it in now! Have you just gone through a period of stagnation and lethargy where nothing seemed to be happening? Let it go! Now is the time of growth. **Eostre** says that wholeness is nurtured when you embrace experiences, risks, and occasions that cause you to stretch. The stretching promotes your growth.

Ritual Suggestion: Growth

Find a time and a place when and where you will not be disturbed. Sit or lie comfortably with your spine straight and close your eyes. Take in a deep breath to the count of six, hold for six, and exhale for six. Do this three times. Let a feeling of relaxation and well-being spread through your body. Now choose a plant. It can be a plant you know well or one you imagine, a cultivated plant or a wild one. You are the seed of this plant, and you have just been placed in the ground by human hands, animal feet, or the breath of the wind. You have been asleep, held in a state of suspended animation until conditions were right for you to begin your cycle of growth. Now it is time for you to wake up and grow. You tingle and vibrate as you begin to expand. Your movement and expansion cause you to break gently out of your hull. You can now begin taking in what you need for your growth.

You drink in moisture from the earth and draw in all that nourishes you. You only take in what you really need and you know what you need. First you develop roots. Those roots travel downward into the earth, both to anchor you and to search for what you need to continue your growth. Now you begin to expand upward, responding to the light and warmth of the sun and you send up your first green leaves. More warmth and light from the sun pulls you up and out. More water and nutrients from the earth, and you grow and create more leaves and deeper roots. As the conditions around you continue to nurture you, you and your environment continue the weaving dance of taking in and expanding out, breathing in and breathing out, as you continue to unfold and become exactly who you are.

Stay with that feeling, sense, or image of breathing in—taking in what you need—and breathing out—expanding and growing—for as long as is appropriate for you. Now take a deep breath and release it slowly, coming back into your human body. When you feel ready, open your eyes. Welcome back!

THE ERINYES

CRISIS

We snap you
crack you
flapjack you
We are that wild chaotic place
that sharp edge
the point that activates your fears
the point of no return
the point where anything can happen
We always demand your death
or complete surrender
you can't get beyond us
around us
or over us
you must meet us and go through us
We are the cosmic steamroller
the place of greatest opportunity
We are crisis

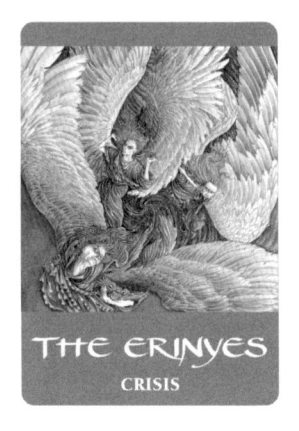

Mythology

The **Erinyes** (pronounced *eh-rin'yees*) were the forces of retribution personified as three immortal dark maiden Goddesses. They took revenge and punished anyone who killed their kin in matriarchal pre-Hellenic Greece. In poet Aeschylus's play, *The Oresteia*, Orestes—the son of Clytemnestra and Agamemnon—kills his mother, thus enraging the **Erinyes** who go after him. When his trial results in a deadlock, Athene, Goddess of wisdom, is called on to cast the deciding vote. Her vote sets Orestes free from any punishment for the matricide. The **Erinyes**, unappeased, demand vengeance. Athene consoles them with promises of special rituals in their honor. They are then renamed the Eumenides, or kindly ones.

Meaning of the Card

The **Erinyes** are howling after you because you and/or a loved one are in crisis. The way to nurture wholeness for you now lies in reaching out and asking for help. Whether it is from the human, animal, or spiritual kingdoms, help is required at this juncture of excess, psyche-breaking stress, and instability. Identify and name the kind of crisis you are in. If your crisis is psychological, call a crisis hot line or make an appointment with a healer of psyches. If your crisis is financial or job-related, seek financial assistance or find a career counselor. If it involves your health, visit a health-care practitioner. It is vital for you to get the help and support you need, for you are not in a place where you can help yourself. Do something. Or ask a friend or loved one to do it for you. Crisis in your life also brings the experience of crisis into the lives of your loved ones. Don't blame yourself or try to take care of them. Be selfish. Deal with your crisis and let them deal with theirs. The **Erinyes** say all crises are accelerated growth/transformation points that bring opportunities. However, before you get to the opportunity, you must get through the crisis, and for that you must reach out for help.

Ritual Suggestion: The Cocoon

The time to do this is now, wherever you are. No time to look for perfect conditions. Use this ritual suggestion to give yourself some breathing space while dancing with your crisis. There is no limit to the number of times you can do the Cocoon.

You can sit or stand anywhere. Close your eyes. Take a deep breath and release it gently. Sense, feel, or see a cocoon being built around you of the most nurturing and comforting materials. Do you like silk or cotton flannel? Does lambswool or a blanket of your favorite flowers soothe you? It could even be a cocoon of rosy pink light or your favorite soothing sounds. Once you have wrapped that cocoon around you, fill it with the love of those who care about you. You can also include animals, plants, stones, the Goddess, trees, the sky, the universe.

Once your cocoon is filled, allow yourself to take the love and comfort of your cocoon into every cell in your body. Feel yourself handing over to the Goddess the challenge that overwhelms you. Feel the comforting sensation as she takes the challenge from you. Keep breathing in the comfort of your cocoon until you feel full. When ready, take a deep breath and exhale gently, open your eyes, and come out of the cocoon. Or you may prefer to stay in it while you go about your tasks in the world. Remember, if you leave it, you can always come right back by taking a deep breath and sensing, feeling, or seeing your cocoon around you.

EURYNOME
ECSTASY

When I awakened and arose
out of swirling seething chaos
seeing no other way to express
the sheer delight
the wild exhilaration
the explosion of energy
I felt
I began to dance my exuberance
that feeling of floating on a sea
of rapturous joy
lost and transported
in the intensity
of ecstasy

Mythology

Eurynome (pronounced *you-reh'no-may*), or "wide wandering," is the Pelasgian (pre-Hellenic peoples of Greece) Great Goddess of all things. She divided the sky from the sea and, while dancing on the waves, created the north wind. The north wind grew lustful, so she seized him in her hands and formed a serpent she called Ophion. **Eurynome** made love with Ophion and then assumed the form of a dove to lay the universal egg out of which all creation came. Ophion, not content with being a creation of **Eurynome** and then cocreating with her, boasted that he was the supreme creator. **Eurynome** knocked out his teeth and banished him.

Meaning of the Card

Eurynome dances into your life to tell you it is time for ecstasy. Ecstasy is here for you in all its fullness, exuberance, and rapture. How can you give yourself ecstasy, that deeply nourishing, intensely joyful place? One way is by healing the wounded parts of yourself. Your wounded parts take up emotional space within you. Once healed, the space they previously occupied becomes available for ecstasy. The more space within, the more room for ecstasy. Another road to ecstasy is to open to it. To give yourself permission to call it in, feel it, and revel in it. For those of us who have experienced little joy in our lives, the conscious decision to court, seduce, and entice ecstasy ensures it will come. **Eurynome** says that when you make the decision to dance with ecstasy, all life challenges you with the opportunities to facilitate that dance.

Ritual Suggestion: Dancing with Eurynome

Find a time and a place when and where you will not be interrupted. Sit or lie comfortably with your spine straight and close your eyes. Take a deep breath and release it slowly. Choose one part of your body to breathe deeply into, and do so. Focus all your attention on that one part, then hold your breath and feel a small pulsing in that body part for a count of five. Slowly exhale and feel, sense, or see your body crumbling into dust while that chosen part is still intact. Now take a deep breath and, as you release it, let that body part crumble into dust.

Visualize, sense, or feel the opening to a cave. It can be a cave

THE GODDESSES

you know or one you've imagined. Take a breath and, as you release it, see yourself standing in front of that cave. Feel the exterior of the cave. Smell the mouth of the cave. Now enter the cave. It is the exact size and temperature it needs to be for you to feel comfortable. Go to the back of the cave, which narrows into a descending tunnel and begin to go down, down, down, deeper and deeper and deeper. Down, down, down, feeling more relaxed, more at ease until you see light at the end of the tunnel. It is a faint, pale gray light and you exit through it. You are now in the great primordial chaos. Nothing is differentiated, everything swirls and seethes. You call out to **Eurynome** and she appears next to you. She invites you to dance ecstasy with her.

Breathe deeply into your heart as you open it to experience what it needs to experience. Take another deep breath, filling your lungs with power and energy. **Eurynome** has begun her dance and the sight, feeling, and sense of it fill you with intense joy, so much so that you feel empowered and inspired to begin your dance. (At this point you may want to turn on some music and begin to dance or you may continue this as a journey.)

You feel joy as you dance. The deliciousness of moving, of being so totally and completely in your body brings you pleasure. The pleasure grows the more you move, the more you express yourself through dance until you feel a vibrant energy hum in your heart. As the hum spreads to your entire body, your heart opens wide to ecstasy and you feel your cells explode. The feeling of dancing is exhilarating, rapturous, ecstatic.

The boundaries of your body dissolve, your very being expands till you feel a sense of union with everything there is, everything there was, everything there will be. You dance and the swirling, seething chaos separates into sky and water. You dance on the waves in total joy and bliss.

Keep on dancing, feeling filled with joy, delight, ecstasy. Keep dancing until you feel full and ready to return. Thank **Eurynome** and return to the cave.

Now you are coming up, up, up, feeling completely refreshed; up, up, up, feeling revitalized, transformed, and vibrantly alive. You reach the cave and walk out through its mouth. Standing outside the cave, take a deep breath and, as you release it, come back into your body. Take another deep breath and open your eyes. Welcome back!

FREYA

SEXUALITY

There was a time
in the beginning
a time when there was nothing
a time when I danced
my dance of sexuality
the energy of creation
and with that dance
gave it to All as my gift
Sexuality brought union with me
with Goddess
with spiritual ecstasy

THE GODDESSES

Sexuality healed and wholed
regenerated and invigorated
Sexuality wove you into the web of all being
life
for life lives to express itself
Whether it be new life
vitality
rites of pleasure
limitless possibility
whatever you choose
sexuality is life's expressive dance
and its greatest gift

Mythology

The northern Europeans called their lusty Goddess **Freya** (pronounced *fray'ya*), which means "mistress," and gave her name to the sixth day of the week, Friday. She was the ruling ancestress of the elder Gods, or Vanir. She and Frigga are two aspects of the Great Goddess, **Freya** being the maiden aspect and Frigga the mother aspect. **Freya** didn't discriminate in her choice of lovers: all the Gods were fair game. When **Freya** appeared draped in her feathered cloak and wearing nothing but her magic amber necklace, none could resist her.

Meaning of the Card

Freya is here to assist you in honoring your sexuality. It is time to connect with that vital, primal, spiritual, regenerating energy and express it, whether or not you have a partner. It's about being fully present in your body. Not just the shoulders or head but the clitoris, anus, breasts, and feet. It's about allowing yourself to feel vibrant, electric energy in your sex organs and use that energy to animate your being.

Have you been feeling that sexuality is too enormous or frightening or taboo to deal with? Do you fear that living and loving your sexuality will keep you from being a "nice girl"? Have the messages learned in your adolescence kept you from exploring your sexuality? (If living your sexuality brings up fear, you may want to work with **Kali:** *Fear,* pp. 94–97, or consult a therapist.) Have you been too busy to take time to give to yourself sexually? Do you feel that sex requires a partner and if you aren't with one you can't enjoy your sexuality? **Freya** says that when you live your sexuality, you open to the dynamic energy that flows through all creation. When you close down, close off, close up, you limit your possibilities for connecting with Goddess energy, which brings you greater vitality. Your path to wholeness needs to include all your parts and your sexuality is an important piece of you.

Ritual Suggestion: Making Love with the Elements

You may either do this as a journey or enact it. If you choose to enact the ritual, you will need to find a place outdoors where you will not be disturbed and where you are assured of privacy. Begin standing, but at any time, feel free to lie or sit. Go slowly and be gentle with yourself. Notice any feelings that come up and breathe with them. Give yourself permission to feel good.

If you choose to do this as a journey, find a time and place where and when you will not be disturbed. Sit or lie down with your spine straight. Take a deep breath and exhale, letting go of all you need to let go of. Take another deep breath, this time through your vulva into your womb. Feel your womb filling with pleasurable sensations. Allow yourself to feel good.

Sense, feel, or see a circle. Go to the east. The east is the place of the element air. In your own words invite the east, the air, to come and play with you. Feel the air caressing your skin, either lightly touching or blowing around and through you in an erotic way. Give over your body to the sensations that are aroused. Allow the air to play with your breasts. Let the air gently stroke your labia, your clitoris. Let the pleasure expand over your entire body. Take your time and allow yourself to experience as much as is appropriate for you.

Then go to the south, the place of the fire. Invite the heat of the sun, the fire, to play with you. Feel the warmth of the sun, the vibrancy of the heat, licking your skin in certain special areas. Then as your pleasure builds, the warmth oozes all over your body. Breathe in the deliciousness caused by the sun, the fire, and let it radiate through your whole body. Take time to experience all that you need.

Move on to the west, the place of the water. Invite the water to play with you. Feel the water as it slips over your skin, caressing you with its moistness. Open your most sensitive places to the water's touch. Allow yourself to feel the pleasure of being with water. Let the water taste you, lick you, enfold you. Breathe in the sensation of the water (not the water itself) and let it surge through your whole body. Take time to experience what you need.

Go to the north, the place of the earth. Invite the earth to come

THE GODDESS ORACLE

and play with you. Take the mud, the thick, moist, earth, and spread it over your body in reverence, in appreciation, honoring the intent to give pleasure to your body. (If you are doing this as a ritual, you may prefer to use baking flour or whatever you consider safe to spread on your genitals.) Spread the earth's love for you thickly and richly over your entire body. Have a good time. Give yourself permission to experiment with whatever arouses you. Let yourself feel the earth making love to you until you feel satisfied. Now take in all the energy you have generated during your lovemaking with the elements. Know that you are in charge of your sexuality and responsible for getting what you need.

When ready, take a deep breath, open your eyes, and return to the here and now. Give thanks to **Freya** for her gift. Welcome back!

GYHLDEPTIS

SYNTHESIS

I take opposites
and conflicts
all that is contradictory
I take the diverse
and varied
I take the simple
and solitary
and mix and merge
meld and blend

THE GODDESSES

I take what is separate
and create union
I bring together
what needs to be brought together
so wholeness is achieved

Mythology

Gyhldeptis (pronounced *gill-dep'tis*), whose name means "lady hanging hair," is the forest Goddess of the Tlingit and Haida people of northwest North America. To her people she was the mossy hanging branches of cedar. When her people were threatened by the destructive whirlpool Kaegyihl Depgeesk, which ate seafaring ships, she called all the natural powers of the coast together and prepared for them a sumptuous feast. Delighted with the feast, they all agreed to work with her. Thus **Gyhldeptis** was able to synthesize their energies and change the whirlpool into a river.

Meaning of the Card

Gyhldeptis glides into your life to tell you the way to wholeness for you now lies in synthesis. It is time to bring all the divergent parts, all the opposing pieces, together into one whole you. At this time in your life you may be engaged in conflict or opposition. Now you must resolve it and create union. Perhaps you are dissipating your energy, your life force, in too many directions or have hundreds of irons in the fire. This is the time to find the common thread that will serve your needs in the best way. **Gyhldeptis** says that by learning to listen to all the different pieces, all the divergent parts of you (and this can include your family, community, partner), you can hear and give what is needed to create wholeness. Wholeness is created when all the parts are honored and listened to, when all the parts are brought together and synthesized into a whole. The greatest gifts to the whole often lie in the most disparate pieces.

Ritual Suggestion: Feasting in Gyhldeptis's Festival House

Find a time and a place when and where you will not be disturbed. Sit or lie comfortably with your spine straight and close your eyes. Take a deep breath and release it with a snake-like "hssssssssss." Now take another deep breath and release it on "haaaaaaaaa." Take another deep breath and release anything and everything that you have not already released. Feel, sense, or see a tunnel. It can be a tunnel you know or one you imagine. It can be a natural tunnel or a human-made one. Take a deep breath and, as you release it, enter the tunnel. It is warm and well lit and you begin to travel down, down, down, deeper and deeper and deeper. You feel comfortable; you feel deeply relaxed as you go down, down, down. You see a light at the end of the tunnel. You step out of the tunnel into the underwater Festival House of **Gyhldeptis**.

She meets you at the entrance and welcomes you into a large dining hall. The dining hall is richly furnished with natural objects. Although the table is set for many, you are the only guest. **Gyhldeptis** seats you in the place of honor. She tells you this is a feast given in your honor, the other places are for all the parts and pieces of yourself.

THE GODDESSES

She asks you to call in all your pieces and you do. ("Calling in" means asking them to come, either by name or by inviting whatever wants or needs to come.) Your pieces arrive and take their seats. You may recognize some of your pieces, some may surprise you, or all may be unknown to you.

With all the places filled at her table, **Gyhldeptis** says that this feast is a magical feast in which all your pieces will be fed what they need so they can synthesize into a whole you. She tells each piece to ask for what it needs. The first piece takes a deep breath and asks for what she needs. It appears and is eaten, accepted, and integrated. Then the next piece asks for what she needs and so on, until all your pieces have asked for what they need, received, eaten, accepted, and integrated it. You are the last to ask for what you need. It appears and you eat it. You feel a surge of power, of energy, of completeness, of wholeness. You stand up and one by one all your pieces move toward you. You embrace them and they become part of you. You feel terrific: vital, energized, centered in your body. Whole. You thank all your pieces and offer your gratitude to **Gyhldeptis**. She thanks you for coming and ushers you to the door.

You enter the tunnel again and begin traveling up, up, up, feeling strong, feeling powerful, feeling whole. Up, up, up, till you reach the entrance of the tunnel and step out. You take a deep breath and, as you release it, you return to your body. When you feel ready, open your eyes. Welcome back!

HATHOR

PLEASURE

When you come to me
I take your spirit
from the stars
and clothe it
in a body of sensation
to finely focus you on form
to benignly bask you in bliss
You are here to experience delight
enjoy gratification
know satisfaction
have pleasure
in all ways
in all modes
in all aspects.
Pleasure makes you juicy
twinkles your eyes
enlivens your life force
The exquisiteness of existence
is pleasure
Get ready to feel soooooooo good

Mythology

Hathor (pronounced *hat'hor*), though depicted in many forms, was mainly associated with the winged cow of creation. As birth and death Goddess, she was credited with creating the body for

THE GODDESSES

the immortal spirit to reside in. As creator of the body, she also governed all bodily pleasures: sound, music, song, dance, art, love, and touch. It was said that she attended the birth of every child and revealed the pattern of its destiny. She was worshipped in Egypt for more than 3,000 years.

Meaning of the Card

Hathor is here to tell you that the way to wholeness for you lies in connecting with what brings you pleasure and in experiencing pleasure. Have you been taught that pleasure is forbidden, something sinful or evil? Are you so busy fulfilling your commitments that pleasure is relegated to the bottom of your list? Do you deny pleasure in order to get work done? STOP! Time to change all that. Pleasure relieves stress and relaxes and refreshes you. Pleasure is the body's way of expressing health and vitality. Pleasure is the oil that keeps you lubricated and lush. **Hathor** says that since you have chosen to be here in a physical body, you might as well enjoy it. Don't wait for others to fulfill this need. Plan to give yourself pleasure daily and you'll find satisfaction dancing in your life.

Ritual Suggestion: The Pleasure Break

This can be done wherever you are, whenever you want, or you can make a special time and place for it in your day. You may do this for as long or as short a time as is appropriate for you.

Take a deep breath and, as you exhale, let yourself relax. Take another deep breath and, as you exhale, give yourself a moment of pleasure. It can be the pleasure of just sitting and breathing. You may choose to take a walk in the woods, bask in the sun, sit in your Sacred Circle of Self (see **Durga**, pp. 56–59), look at a painting, read a book, or listen to music—anything that brings you pleasure. Whatever it is, give it to yourself, either in actuality or through visualization. What gives you pleasure may change over time. If you don't know what gives you pleasure, then sit with it, open to it, be receptive to finding it, then give it to yourself.

HECATE

CROSSROADS

I sit in the blackness of the
    dark moon night
with my hounds
at the crossroads
where three roads converge
at the crossroads
the place of choice
All paths lead to the crossroads
and all are desirable
but only one can you travel
only one can you choose
choice creates endings
and all beginnings come from endings
at the crossroads
Which one will you choose?
which way will you go?
which?
Though the choice is yours

THE GODDESSES

here's a secret I'll share
The way to choose is to enter the void
the way to choose is to let die
the way to choose is to fly free

Mythology

Hecate (pronounced *he–ka'tay*) is considered by some to be a Thracian moon Goddess and by others to be an ancient pre-Greek Goddess of midwives, birth, fertility, the dark of the moon, magic, wealth, education, ceremonies, and the Underworld. Worshipped at the places where three roads crossed, she would walk abroad on nights when the moon was dark, attended by a pack of hounds. People honored her by leaving offerings at the crossroads. As crone she also formed a triad with Persephone (maiden) and **Demeter** (mother).

Meaning of the Card

Hecate meets you at the crossroads when you must make a choice. Times of choice are not easy times. The challenges presented by choice necessitate a leap of faith from the person doing the choosing. **Hecate** says to let go of the idea that there are wrong or right choices: there is just choice. Have you been putting off making a choice because it seems to be too overwhelming or a "no win" situation? Does the choice bring up fear of the unknown? Does it seem better and/or easier to remain with what you know?

Sometimes a choice must be made, yet you are not ready. In such cases, the way to nurture wholeness is to acknowledge where you are and let it go. Trust that you will be able to make a choice when the time is right. Give yourself time and space. Don't press, berate, or blame yourself. You need nourishment here. When you let go, suddenly clarity comes to show you what you need. **Hecate** urges you to embrace the unknown. Know that whatever you choose will bring you something invaluable that you can use on your path to wholeness.

Ritual Suggestion: Hecate's Journey of Perspective

Find a time and place when and where you will not be disturbed. Sit or lie comfortably with your spine straight. When you feel ready, close your eyes. Take a deep breath and release it slowly. Take another deep breath and, as you release it, let your body fall as if you were removing a suit of silk clothes, letting it lie in a pool at your feet. Take another deep breath and see, sense, or feel **Hecate**, the ancient one, the crone Goddess, standing in front of you. She holds out her hand and you take it.

A path appears before you and you both step onto it. The path is of black stone, large chunks of obsidian, and it leads you in a spiral descent. You go down, down, down, deeper and deeper and deeper, spiraling on the obsidian path with **Hecate** by your side. Her presence is reassuring and comforting. You continue to spiral downward on the obsidian path until you reach a crossroads. There the path of black stone is met by a path of pearl (or white stone) and a path of coral (or red stone).

All the paths reach out to you. Which one you will travel? They are all enticing and all promise something you need. Ask **Hecate** for help in choosing.

THE GODDESSES

At the place where the three paths intersect, **Hecate** sits down and motions for you to sit next to her. As you sit, you are aware of the power of the intersecting paths vibrating beneath you. You take a deep breath and feel the vibrations in your body. The vibrations increase so that they are like gusts of wind sweeping through you. They wash you clean of everything. They engulf you, surround you, hold you. The vibrating gusts of wind help you to let go of everything: thoughts, feelings, doings. **Hecate** is with you should you need any assistance.

The winds envelope you and you begin to fly with them. They take you swinging from side to side, and then up and down. **Hecate** flies with you. As the winds take you up, up, up, **Hecate** suggests you notice the three paths below you. They no longer entice or dazzle. They seem small and insignificant. Just three paths, three possibilities.

The winds die down and you gently float to the ground. It is time to return. You take **Hecate**'s hand and she leads you up, up, up, the spiral path, the path of obsidian. Up, up, up you spiral, feeling energized and deeply relaxed, feeling calm and centered, until you reach the end of the path. **Hecate** embraces you and you thank her for the journey, the gift of perspective and clarity. She asks you for something and you give it to her with gratitude. **Hecate** vanishes and you take a deep breath. As you exhale you return to your body. Take another deep breath and when ready, open your eyes. Welcome back!

HESTIA

HEARTH/HOME

I am what's at the core
the indescribable
the elusive
the living presence
that inhabits and transforms
a building
a dwelling
an edifice
taking it from the realm of
marble
stone
or wood
and with its hearth fire lit
making it a home

Mythology

Hestia (pronounced *hess'tee-ya*) is so ancient a Goddess that she is invoked by simply lighting a fire in your hearth. She was central to civilization because she represented the center of the home, the community, the town, the city. No meal could be eaten without her, for she was the very fire that transformed the ingredients into nourishment. Conscripted into the Olympian pantheon, eldest Goddess **Hestia** gave up her seat and went to tend the hearth so the new God of ecstasy and wine, Dionysus, could be seated.

THE GODDESSES

Meaning of the Card

Hestia has come to tend her hearth fire in your life and to tell you it is time to focus on home. Whether you are living alone, with your family, or with friends, it is time to make your home a priority. Perhaps you are living in a house that is not your home or with people you don't want to live with. Perhaps your home is filled with so many others that you have no space of your own. Perhaps your life is such a busy whirlwind that your dwelling is not your home, merely a place to change clothes and sleep. Now is the time to come home. **Hestia** says that wholeness is nurtured when you learn to come home to yourself and then to create the appropriate physical manifestation: a home that will nurture you.

Ritual Suggestion: Coming Home

Find a time and a place where and when you will not be disturbed. Sit or lie comfortably with your spine straight and close your eyes. Focus your awareness on your toes and breathe into them. Allow yourself to feel present in your toes. How does that feel? Now expand your awareness to your feet and breathe into them. Again, what does that feel like? Expand your awareness to include your legs, and breathe. Check in with yourself about how that feels. Continue expanding your awareness to include your pelvis, womb, abdomen, inner organs, and so on, until gradually you are fully aware of your entire body. Take a deep breath into all the parts of your body and, as you release it, allow yourself to feel really present, at home in your body. Take more deep breaths experiencing this sense of "at homeness," this presence in your body. Take as much time as you need to savor the feeling.

For Women Who Need a Home of Their Own

Continue after "Coming Home." Keeping your eyes closed, see, sense, or feel your ideal home. Is it an apartment in a city or a log cabin in the woods? Is it a palatial estate or a cozy nest? Whatever brings you pleasure and joy, create it for yourself. Do you need to build it brick by brick or just wave your magic wand? Does it sit amid formal English gardens, a field of wildflowers, acres of desert, or rocks and cliffs? Create it according to what you need. It can always change if you want it to. This is your spirit home, your home away from home, your place to come home to whenever you choose. It is there for you when you need it.

INANNA

EMBRACING THE SHADOW

I went there
of my own free will
I went there
in my finest gown
with my rarest jewels
and my Queen of Heaven crown
In the Underworld
at each of the seven gates
I was stripped seven times
of all that I thought I was
till I stood bare in who I really am
Then I saw Her

THE GODDESSES

She was huge and dark and smelly and hairy
with a lion's head
and lion's claws
devouring everything before Her
Ereskigal, my sister
She was all that I am not
All that I have hidden
All that I have buried
She is what I have denied.
Ereskigal, my sister
Ereskigal, my shadow
Ereskigal, my self

Mythology

Sumerian Queen of Heaven, **Inanna** (pronounced *eh-na'na*) tricked her father, Enki, God of Wisdom, into giving her the hundred objects of culture, which she then gave to humankind. Desiring to pay a visit to her sister, Ereskigal, she journeyed to the Underworld. There she was stripped and killed, and left to hang on a hook for three days and three nights. **Inanna** was allowed to leave the Underworld only if she found a substitute. She chose her son-lover, the shepherd Damuzi, who, in her absence, had usurped her place on the throne of Heaven.

Meaning of the Card

Inanna is here to tell you that a journey to the Underworld is the way to wholeness for you now. It is time to dance with your shadow, reclaim what you've denied, embrace your own Dark

Sister/Dark Self. You need all those aspects of yourself that your parents, caregivers, teachers, society have deemed unacceptable in order to achieve wholeness in your life. Whether it be your talent, your beauty, your inner vampire, your anger, your madness, you are required to surrender to the journey and embrace your dark side. If you are already in the Underworld, the appearance of **Inanna** may signal that the time for your return is at hand. Journeys to the Underworld to embrace your dark side are a law unto themselves. They take as much time as they need to take—you can't just fit them into your schedule. When it is time for you to journey, you will and you will not be done until you return. Take comfort in the fact that all journeys to the Underworld do end and that you will indeed return—much different from who you thought you were when you went.

Ritual Suggestion: Journey to Meet Your Shadow

Find a time and place when and where you will not be disturbed. Sit or lie comfortably with your back straight. When you feel ready, take a deep breath and release it, letting everything go. Breathe in and let your body relax. As you breathe out, drop your body as if you were removing a suit of silk clothes, letting it lie in a pool at your feet. Breathe in and see the entrance to a tunnel. It can be one you are familiar with or one you invent. As you breathe out, see yourself standing before it. Breathe in and enter. The tunnel is warm and well lit. You begin to go down, down, down. The tunnel is safe and feels pleasant. You are going down, down, down, deeper and deeper and deeper. Now you see a light at the end of the tunnel. You are at the threshold of the Underworld. Step out into the Underworld.

THE GODDESSES

Call what you need to see—your shadow, your dark side. Call this entity to you and it will come. What does it look like? How does it make you feel? It asks you for something and you give it freely. (*Note:* If you experience any fear, either before the journey or when you meet your shadow, keep breathing deeply and acknowledge the fear. It is there to help you. Being able to witness all the parts/aspects of ourselves, with or without fear, is what brings us to wholeness.)

It is now time to return, so bid your shadow good-bye for now and return to the tunnel. Now you are coming up, up, up, through the warmth and the safety of the tunnel, feeling energized, feeling refreshed, feeling relaxed. Up, up, up, till you reach the entrance of the tunnel. Take a deep breath and, when you exhale, you are back in your body. Take a deep breath and, when you exhale, if ready, open your eyes. Welcome back!

ISIS

MOTHERING

I conceived
carried
and birthed all life
Then, out of my love for you
my children
I gave you my beloved mate, Osiris
Lord of vegetation
God of the grain

to be cut down
and born again
I nursed you through sickness with my healing arts
I made you clothes and invented weaving and spinning
I watched over your first steps
helping you grow from infancy to maturity
I was even there with you
at the end
to hold your hand
and guide you to immortality
You were All
and I gave you all
and to you I was All
Isis, Great Goddess, All Mother

Mythology

Isis (pronounced *eye'sis*), also know as Au Set ("exceeding queen") and Isis Panthea ("Isis the All-Goddess"), was worshipped in many places including Egypt, the Roman Empire, Greece, and Germany. When her beloved Osiris was killed then dismembered and scattered by her brother Set, **Isis** searched out the pieces and reassembled them. She found all but his penis, which she replaced with one of gold. Through use of her magic and healing arts she brought Osiris back to life then conceived, through his golden penis, the Sun God Horus. When the temples of **Isis** were turned into Christian churches, **Isis** with baby Horus on her lap became the Virgin Mary and Jesus.

THE GODDESSES

Meaning of the Card

Isis has appeared in your life to tell you it is time for mothering. Have you been giving all your mothering energy away without keeping some for yourself? Have you taken on a new project or just had a new baby? Do you feel that something needs extra mothering, but you aren't up to it? Did your own mother or caregiver give you the mothering you needed? **Isis** says that it is important to get the mothering you need in order to heal past wounds. Everyone needs to be mothered, regardless of whether you are a maiden, mother, or crone.

Ritual Suggestion: Journey to Isis

Find a time and a place when and where you will not be disturbed. Sit or lie comfortably with your spine straight and close your eyes. Take a deep breath and release it with the sound "ma." Take another deep breath and let go of all you are holding onto as you sound "ma." Now take a deep breath and, as you release it see, sense, or feel yourself on a smooth clear river in a small boat. It is a warm, sunny day and the boat is rocking you gently back and forth, back and forth, back and forth. You lie in the boat on soft cushions while the boat carries you along. Allow yourself to surrender to the warmth of the sun and the motion of the boat. The sounds of the water lapping against the boat send you into a blissfully relaxed state. You are now able to ask "where do I need mothering?" You see, feel, or sense a time in your life, past or present, when you needed to be mothered and didn't receive what you needed. Allow any feelings that come up to be expressed.

The boat drifts into a landing and stops. You sit up. Before you is the Temple of **Isis**. You get out of the boat and walk up to the Temple. Take off your shoes and enter the Temple. It is dark inside, except for an oil lamp which burns in the entryway. You take the oil lamp and continue into the depths of **Isis**'s temple. Find a spot where you feel comfortable and put the oil lamp on the ground, then sit before it and call **Isis**.

Isis appears and asks you what you need. You tell her of the time in your life when you needed mothering and ask her to mother you. Give yourself over to her and take in her divine mothering, till you feel full and satiated. **Isis** asks you for a gift and you give it to her with an open heart.

When you are ready to leave, thank her. **Isis** vanishes and you pick up the oil lamp, return it to its place, and leave the temple. The boat is waiting for you. You get back into the boat. The boat drifts out into the river and heads back. You drift with it feeling relaxed, revitalized, and at peace. The boat lands on the opposite side of the river. Take a deep breath, release it slowly and, when you feel ready, open your eyes. Welcome back!

THE GODDESSES

IX CHEL

CREATIVITY

I weave strings of energy
into the web of creation
Where nothing was before
out of the void
into the world
I spin them into existence
Out from my mind
out from my body
out of my awareness of what needs to be
Now there is something new
and all life is nourished

Mythology

Ix Chel (pronounced *e'shell*) was worshipped by the Maya of the Yucatan peninsula on Cozumel, her sacred island. The Moon/Snake Goddess, she helps assure fertility by holding the sacred womb jar upside down so that the waters of creation can be ever flowing. **Ix Chel** also presides over weaving, magic, health and healing, sexuality, water, and childbirth. The dragonfly is her special animal. When she was almost killed by her grandfather for becoming the Sun's lover, the dragonfly sang over her until she was well.

Meaning of the Card

Ix Chel has woven herself into your life to tell you it is time to express creativity. It is time to stoke the fire, time to let your creative energy flow. Create! Be daring! But also be responsible and conscious, whether your creations are works of art or works of the flesh (children). Creativity nurtures, creativity reweaves the tears in our vitality, creativity heals. It is our birthright and our life blood; it makes us healthy and happy. We women have the ability to create: we give birth. So find the time, make the time, create the time to be creative. Beat that drum, use those paints, make that pottery, put on those dancing shoes, write those novels, explore your sexuality, rejoice in your own creativity. Create in the way that is appropriate for you. Let nothing stop you.

Do you feel blocked creatively because you aren't as good as someone else? Do the kids, your partner, your family, your job keep you from being creative? Stop using your creativity to find reasons not to create. **Ix Chel** says wholeness is nurtured when you open to your creativity and live it.

Ritual Suggestion: Ix Chel's Energy Web

Find a time and a place when and where you will not be disturbed. You may wish to do this just before you go to sleep. Sit or lie comfortably with your spine straight and close your eyes. Take a deep breath and release it slowly through your mouth without making a sound. Take another deep breath and let all the stress and tension in your body/mind/spirit leave you as vapor and disappear. Allow yourself to relax deeply. In that state of relaxation feel, sense, or envision the atoms in your body vibrating. Now extend that awareness to your bed. The bed is comprised of atoms and they are vibrating, dancing. Let yourself become one with your bed, just molecules of vibrating energy. Now extend that awareness to your room, then your house or apartment, then your city. Each time you extend the awareness you feel, all the other energies becoming one mass of vibrating energy.

Extend your awareness to your region or state, then your country, your hemisphere, this planet. All is pure vibrating energy. Now you are a piece of energy vibrating in the solar system. You feel, sense, see yourself as a piece of vibrating energy in the energy web called the universe. Be in that place for as long as is appropriate for you.

When you are ready, feel what you want to create. Feel it as vividly as possible. What do you want to create? Is it a new home? a different career? a painting, musical composition, book, piece of pottery, theater piece, relationship? Create it responsibly and consciously. Feel the new strand, your creation, being added to the energy web, then surround it in energy and let it go.

Now it is time for you to come back. Beginning with a piece of energy vibrating in the universe, contract your energy field to a piece of energy vibrating in the solar system, then Earth, your hemisphere, your country, your region, city, apartment or house, then your room, your bed. Now you are in your body, doing your energy dance alone, just you. When you are ready, open your eyes. Welcome back!

KALI

FEAR

I am the dance of death that is
    behind all life
the ultimate horror
the ultimate ecstasy
I am existence
I am the dance of destruction that
    will end this world
the timeless void
the formless devouring mouth
I am rebirth
Let me dance you to death
Let me dance you to life
Will you walk through your fears to dance with me?
Will you let me cut off your head
and drink your blood?
then will you cut off mine?
Will you face all the horror
all the pain
all the sorrow
and say "yes"?
I am all that you dread
all that terrifies
I am your fears
will you meet me?

THE GODDESSES

Mythology

Kali (pronounced *kah'lee*), the Hindu triple Goddess of creation, preservation, and destruction, is the animating force of Shiva, the destroyer (Lord of the Dance). She is the insatiable hunger of time that births then devours. Skulls, cemeteries, and blood are all associated with her worship. **Kali**'s energy is uncontrollable. After killing two demons, she got drunk on their blood and began dancing on their dead flesh. She danced herself into a frenzy until she realized she almost danced Shiva to death.

Meaning of the Card

Kali has begun her dance in your life to tell you it is time to face your fears. All that is lurking ominously, either buried deep in your inner darkness or close by, needs to be stared in the eye and brought into the light of consciousness. Are your fears serving you by warning you about dangerous places, things, or people? Or do your fears prevent you from dancing your dance, living your life, creating with Creation? **Kali** comes to tell you that your dance is needed as part of the whole Dance of Creation. Wholeness is nurtured when you reclaim the pieces of yourself that you've given over to fear. Most fears are formless. By naming and witnessing the fear, you gain power. Wholeness is created when you learn to acknowledge your fears and walk through them.

Ritual Suggestion: Meeting Your Fear

Find a time and place when and where you will not be disturbed. Sit or lie comfortably with your spine straight and close your eyes. When you feel ready, take a deep breath and release it, letting everything go. Breathe in and let your body relax. As you breathe out, drop your body like a suit of silk clothes, letting it lie in a pool around you. Place your hand over your heart so that you can feel the rhythm and pulse of your heartbeat. Let the rhythm of your breath slow down as you breathe in and out, listening to your heartbeat. Take a deep breath and, as you exhale, see yourself standing inside your heart. It feels very comfortable.

There is a path behind your heart known as the "hidden path." Step onto that path. The path takes you up and it takes you down. The path takes you over and it takes you under. On the path you experience all you need to experience and you see all you need to see. The path begins to climb gradually up, up, up. Now the path has become steep and you are required to climb hand over hand until you reach a ledge. You pull yourself up onto the ledge and slowly stand up.

You are now on the Plain of Vision, where the winds blow cool, clear, and clean—where you can see all you need to see. Take a deep breath and inhale the clarity of the Plain of Vision.

You are now ready to call your fear. You call your fear and it comes. When you meet your fear, ask its name and it will tell you. What does it look like? Notice any feelings you are having and breathe into them. Your fear asks you for something and you give it freely.

It is now time to return. Ask your fear to accompany you and abide by its decision. Take another full, deep breath of the clarity of the Plain of Vision. Return to the ledge and begin the climb down, down, down. The path takes you down and it takes you under. You are feeling refreshed and revitalized, feeling light and buoyant as you return on the hidden path that lies behind your heart.

THE GODDESSES

You approach your heart and step into it, experiencing the pulsing of your blood. Take a deep breath and, when you exhale, you are back in your body. Take a deep breath and, when you exhale, if ready, open your eyes. Welcome back!

KUAN YIN
COMPASSION

I made the vow
and kept my word
I reached enlightenment
but rather than pass over
to the state of eternal bliss
I retained human form
till all beings attain enlightenment
Keeping human form
enabled me to know more deeply
the pain others experience
Because of my deep feelings
because of my understanding
of misery and suffering
because of my decision
I am called The Compassionate One
She Whose Name Alleviates All Suffering
But wouldn't you prefer to wait
feeling what others feel
suffering what others suffer

knowing their pain as your own
wait till the end of all suffering and pain
till all beings attain enlightenment?
For me there was no other choice

Mythology

Kuan Yin (pronounced *koo-wan'yin*), or "she who hears the weeping world," is the Chinese Buddhist bodhisatva of Compassion. She lives on her island paradise of P'u T'o Shan where she is said to grant every prayer she hears. She is so powerful that even the mention of her name will ease suffering and hardship. Choosing to remain in this world after having attained enlightenment, **Kuan Yin** has vowed to retain human form until all beings attain enlightenment. In Japan she is known as Kwannon.

Meaning of the Card

Kuan Yin appears mercifully in your life to tell you it is time to nurture wholeness with compassion—compassion for others, compassion for your loved ones, compassion for yourself. Do you find yourself feeling irritated or apathetic to the suffering of others? What keeps you from your compassion? Do you allow yourself space and ease when you are less than your idea of perfect? Do you find yourself wanting to hurt others because you have been hurt? Do you fear opening your heart to the plight of others because it will hurt you? Compassion is the ability to listen deeply and allow others and yourself the space to go through what needs to be gone through and to feel what needs to be felt. **Kuan Yin** says that the way to alleviate your suffering is to develop compassion for yourself. From that compassionate place within, you can manifest compassion without.

Ritual Suggestion: Journey to Kuan Yin

Find a time and a place when and where you will not be disturbed. Sit or lie comfortably with your spine straight and close your eyes. Take a deep breath and release it slowly. Then take another breath, breathing deeply into your heart, and release it slowly while feeling your heart expand. Take a deep breath and release it with a sigh from your heart. See, sense, or feel yourself inside your heart. Hear your heartbeat pulsing around you. Inside your heart is a rainbow bridge. You step onto the rainbow bridge and begin to cross the great waters. As you travel the bridge, you become more and more relaxed. The great waters are serene and calming, the bridge itself is a delight to walk on, the air is refreshing and pleasant.

On the other side of the rainbow bridge lies **Kuan Yin**'s island paradise of P'u T'o Shan. She greets you as you arrive and hands you a beautiful flower. As you inhale the flower's fragrance, you feel your heart open. She takes you by the hand and leads you through the rich, lush, fragrant vegetation to her pavilion. After seating you with care and consideration, she washes your feet then serves you what you need to be served. She asks you to tell her your troubles and you do. She listens deeply and attentively. You feel nourished and loved at the very core of your being. You feel completely and utterly heard, seen, listened to. It feels wonderful and deeply healing. You feel lighter and more at ease with yourself. Sit with **Kuan Yin** until you are ready to return. She takes you back to the rainbow bridge and embraces you. You thank her and begin your way across the bridge, feeling recharged and revitalized. The trip back across the rainbow bridge is short and you arrive back in your heart. Take a deep breath and, as you release it, you come back into your body. Take another deep breath and, as you release it, open your eyes. Welcome back!

LADY OF BEASTS

RELATIONSHIP

I desire union
in ways comfortable and appropriate
I open to the dance with another
knowing that it will take me
to all the places I fear
some of the places I love
many of the places that need healing.
I listen with the ears of my heart
and communicate from a place of self-knowing
I consciously give myself away
and know how to take myself back
I see myself reflected
so perfectly in the other
that I begin my most important journey:
to seek out and claim
more of who I am

THE GODDESSES

Mythology

The Goddess as **Lady of Beasts** was known to the people of Sumer, Crete, and the Indus Valley (India). Her name is largely unknown because worship of her predated writing. She was also known as the Cosmic Creatrix, the creative, fertile, life-giving force. Her special animals were held sacred as manifestations of the deity herself. She is depicted here pregnant, surrounded by pregnant animals, which speaks of her as a powerful fertility figure. She usually appears enthroned with a lion at her side indicating sovereignty and strength.

Meaning of the Card

Lady of Beasts walks slowly and serenely into your life to tell you it is time to focus on creating supportive and nurturing relationships, with your unborn child, the animal(s) in your life, a lover, family, friends, and/or coworkers. Relating to others enables you to look at the parts of yourself that you don't ordinarily see. Relationships are the mirror in which you can see who you really are. Wholeness is nourished when you see who you really are, accept what you see, and strive to heal what needs to be healed.

Are you in a relationship that presses all your buttons, brings up all your issues, leaves you feeling like a "woman on the verge of a nervous breakdown"? If both (or all) of you are committed to doing the work, willing to accept your pieces, your responsbility, this could be a gold mine. Perhaps you are in an abusive relationship, one that keeps hurting and hurting with no redeeming factors or one in which your partner is not looking at issues. This could be the time to gather your strength, lick your wounds, and move on. Perhaps better communication or acceptance could help your relationship. If you are contemplating a relationship, this is the time to open and engage. **Lady of Beasts** says the dance of relationship is the fast track to evolving consciousness and personal power. It is joyful, painful, frustrating, exhilarating, annihilating, and completely worth it.

Ritual Suggestion: Creating Win-Win Situations

Find a time and a place when and where you and your partner, coworker, family member, or friend can be with each other uninterrupted. If the other person is not available to do this with you, you can do this as a journey on your own. You will need something that can serve as a "talking stick or stone."* You and the other(s) should be clear on what you all need, so that each of you can state that need clearly. Creating win-win situations brings all parties together to negotiate for those needs so that everyone wins. If there is any emotion around a need or if some feelings come up during the ritual, those emotions and/or feelings will need to be dealt with before a win-win situation can be achieved. (See **Demeter:** *Feelings/Emotions,* pp. 53–56.)

To create sacred space you can do a full ritual of calling in the elements/directions, burning incense, inviting in your

---

*An object held by one person at a time, signifying that s/he alone has the privilege of speaking. All present have the privilege of listening in a respectful way until that person is finished talking. When that person is finished, s/he passes the "stick" to the next person and so on, till all have a chance to express themselves and be heard.

power animals, the Goddess and God, and/or other spirit guides; or you can invoke the spirit of cooperation and completion. It is up to you. Remember to do what is appropriate and respectful for all.

Once sacred space has been created, it is time to pass the talking object. Each person states his or her needs, then you come to an agreement. For example: You want to go roller-skating on Thursday nights and need your partner to watch the kids. Your partner wants to go to science club meetings on Tuesday nights and wants you to watch the kids. You agree to watch the kids on Tuesday nights if he will watch them on Thursdays. This is a win-win situation.

There may be situations where you will have to do more negotiation, and possibly some compromise, in order for everyone's needs to be met. It is important to really sit with any proposed compromise. Only you can decide if you can compromise, and in some cases you may not be able to. Not all situations can be resolved in a win-win way. There may be times when you give, the other person gives, and you both give. Relationships are a balancing act. The more you strive to create win-win situations, the more often you will succeed.

LAKSHMI

ABUNDANCE

I am the ever-flowing outpouring
  of plenty
the inexhaustible
the never ending
from the fullness of my being
I give richly and opulently
generously and copiously
luxuriously and liberally
I am limitless
for I cannot be contained
I am everywhere
and will never cease to be

Mythology

Worship of **Lakshmi** (pronounced *lock'shmee*) began prior to the Aryan invasion of India. She is considered the animating force or Shakti of Vishnu, the Preserver. Her sacred animal is the cow, symbol of abundance and plenty. She appears here with elephants pouring water, another symbol of her powerful abundance. Although described as floating on the eternal sea of time, resting on a lotus, Hindus say that the Gods churned the sea of creation from which **Lakshmi** appeared in all her splendor.

Meaning of the Card

Lakshmi appears in your life to tell you it is time to nurture wholeness by recognizing and living from abundance. Is your

THE GODDESSES

existence defined and contained by the parameters of scarcity rather than abundance? Are your finances based on a poverty consciousness rather than limitlessness and plenty? Is your outlook on life one of never having enough rather than of having your needs met? Let yourself open to the abundance, the bounty that exists in your world. **Lakshmi** says that abundance is hard to perceive if lack, poverty, and scarcity dominate your consciousness. The way to wholeness for you lies in opening to the flow of abundance in the universe and recognizing the abundance in your life. When you open to the flow, you become part of it and you draw it to you. When you become aware of the abundance in your life in all its forms—friendship, health, family, love, beauty, talent, humor, et cetera—you can call in more from a conscious place.

Ritual Suggestion: Flowing with Lakshmi

Find a time and a place when and where you will not be disturbed. You will need paper and a pen. Make a list of all that you have in your life. For example: a home, lover(s), friends, children, food, talent, beauty, clothes, health, animals, et cetera. When you've finished your list, sit or lie with your spine straight and close your eyes. Take a deep breath and exhale. As you take another deep breath, allow yourself to inhale sweet-smelling golden energy. As you exhale, this sweet-smelling golden energy circulates throughout your body. Do this again. Now feel, sense, or see the entrance to a tunnel: it can be one you know or one you imagine. Enter that tunnel. The tunnel is pleasant and well lit, and as you move through it your relaxation deepens.

At the end of the tunnel is a path. The path takes you to an enormous lotus pond. On the banks of the lotus pond are sumptuous cushions, the most luxurious clothing you have ever seen, and some exquisite jewelry. Put on the clothes and jewels, and seat yourself on the cushions. Food and drink appear before you in an inexhaustible supply.

When you have made yourself comfortable and refreshed yourself, turn your gaze to the pond. As you watch the pond, a huge lotus flower begins to open, revealing **Lakshmi** in all her splendor. She asks for your list and you hand it to her. You give thanks to her for the abundance you have in your life and ask her for abundance in the area where you need it. She asks you to hand over to her a tangible physical symbol to represent that area of your life. As you give it to her, you feel a tremendous sense of relief. You experience the luxury of knowing that she is taking care of that aspect of your life. It is now time for you to return. You bid **Lakshmi** good-bye and thank her. She tells you to keep the clothes and jewels. As she speaks, the clothing and jewelry dissolve and become part of you. You are left with the sensation that you are still beautifully attired. Now you follow the path back to the tunnel. You return through the well-lit and comfortable tunnel. You leave the tunnel and take a deep breath and, as you release it, you return to your body. When you feel ready, open your eyes. Welcome back!

LILITH

POWER
I dance my life for myself
I am whole
I am complete

THE GODDESSES

I say what I mean
and I mean what I say
I dance the dark and the light
the conscious and the unconscious
the sane and the insane
and I speak from myself
authentically
with total conviction
without regard for how I might look
All the parts of myself
flow into the whole
all my divergent selves unite as one
I listen
to what needs to be heard
I never make excuses
I feel my feelings
deeply and profoundly
I never hide
I live my sexuality
to please myself
and pleasure others
I express it as it needs to be expressed
from the core of myself
from the wholeness of my dance
I am female
I am sexual
I am power
I was greatly feared.

LILITH
POWER

Mythology

Lilith (pronounced *lil'ith*) was originally the Sumerian Queen of Heaven, a Goddess older than **Inanna**. The Hebrews took the Goddess and transformed her into the first wife of Adam, who refused to lie beneath him when having intercourse. She insisted that because they were created equal, they needed to have sex equally. When Adam refused, she left him. Thereafter, in Jewish mythology, she was described as a demon.

Meaning of the Card

Lilith appears to tell you to take back your power. Where are the places you have lost or given away your power? What beliefs do you hold that deny your power? Have you been told that powerful women never find mates? Or that women can't have power because that would make them unfeminine? Have you been teased, shunned, ostracized by others when you've stepped into your power? Are you afraid of misusing your power to dominate or manipulate? **Lilith** says that the way to wholeness for you now lies in acknowledging that you're not connecting with your power, then second coming to terms with and accepting your power.

Ritual Suggestion: Cord-cutting Ceremony

You may do this ritual suggestion at any time. Working with the lunar cycles will increase its power. A good time to cut cords is at the dark of the moon. The time to put on the cords is the day after the full moon. You may wear the cords till the new moon or keep them on for a longer or shorter period—whatever feels right for you.

THE GODDESSES

You will need rope, yarn, string, or whatever feels right. It should be sturdy enough for you to wear for the length of time you have chosen. You will also need a pair of scissors, a knife, and an incense burner, cauldron, or wood-burning stove. You can do this alone or with others.

Preparation: Choose up to three ways you have not been in your power. Perhaps you've been afraid of stepping into your power or your beliefs keep you from expressing your power. Next decide on a date to put on the cords. It could be right now or you might want to align with the cycles of the moon. When you have decided on your date, assemble all the things listed above.

Ceremony: You may cast a circle or do whatever is appropriate for you. When ready, pick up your cord and cut it to the length desired. The length you choose will be determined by where on your body you plan to tie it, for example, your ankles, wrists, throat, or waist. The place you choose will be determined by what the cord represents. If you want to transform what keeps you from walking in your power, you might tie cords around your ankles. If you have trouble speaking your truth, you might choose your throat. If fear of your sexuality keeps you from your power, you might tie the cord low around your hips. Do what feels right.

As you are tying the cord next to your skin, speak the meaning of the cord. For example, "This cord symbolizes my desire to be in my power by speaking my own truth." When finished, go on to the next cord. You may choose to work with only one cord at a time or you may work with three. Be sure you can give attention to all the cords. During the days leading up to the cord-cutting, you will need to focus on each cord and what it represents by looking at the cord or feeling it next to your skin.

On the day or night you have chosen to cut the cords, have the incense burner, cauldron or wood-burning stove, matches, and a knife or scissors ready. You may cast a circle or do whatever is appropriate for you. When ready, light whatever you are using. Do you want to dance and drum wildly, shout the meaning of the cord and how you take your power back as you cut the cord? Or do you prefer to sit quietly, state the meaning of the cord and your desire to take back your power, then cut the cord? Do what is appropriate for you. You may want to cut each cord differently. Cut the first cord, go on to the next, till all the cords are cut. Now take the cords and put them in your incense burner, cauldron, or wood-burning stove and watch them burn. Allow yourself to feel a surge of power as you watch each cord turn to smoke.

If you want to dance, let your dance symbolize your intention to take back power and whatever the cord means to you. When finished with your dance, cut your cords and put them in the fire.

If you are doing this with a group, the group can drum or play music. Each member will have time in the center of the circle dancing her cords. When she is done with her dance, she can cut the cords herself or designate another to cut them. She places them in the fire and when they have burned, it is the next person's turn till everyone has danced, cut her cords, and burned them.

Take a deep breath and feel your new sense of power. If you have cast a circle, release what you have called in with gratitude. Give thanks to **Lilith** for pointing the way to your own power.

MAAT

JUSTICE

I am the law of truth
the path of integrity
preserver of the code
and in my heart justice lives
I weigh all deeds against
my feather of truth
I weigh all deeds
and should they prove the heavier
then I give the lessons
I create the opportunities
I open the pathways
I graciously bestow
that which needs to be learned
to right all wrongs

Mythology

Maat (pronounced *maht*) was an ancient Egyptian Goddess of law, order, truth, and justice. With her feather of truth she weighed the souls of all who came to her subterranean Hall of Judgment. She would place her plume on her scales opposite the heart of the deceased. If the scales balanced, the deceased could feast with deities and spirits of the dead; if the heart was heavy, the deceased was turned over to Ahemait (Underworld Goddess who is part hippopotamus, part lion, part crocodile) to be devoured.

Meaning of the Card

Maat has come with her feather of truth to assist you in bringing justice into your life. Are you in a situation that seems unfair, unjust, unreasonable? Have you used integrity, yet another or others have not, and now you are wounded and seek justice? Have you not been honest in your words, your deeds, your actions? Are you being unjust to others? to yourself? Perhaps your standards are so rigid that you find them impossible to meet and continually need to rebel? Do you have an inner judge who condemns you for any infractions in his/her rule? Now is the time to look at your life and invite justice in. Now is the time to repay all debts, to strike a fair and reasonable balance in all your dealings. **Maat** says that the way to wholeness for you lies in accepting the loving nature of justice which seeks to right all wrongs by administering the lessons needed.

Ritual Suggestion: Handing Over to Maat for Justice

Find a time and a place where and when you will not be disturbed. You may want to wear clothing that is different from your everyday apparel. You may want to light some incense and/or candles. Do what is most comfortable for you.

Cast your circle by calling in or becoming the elements earth, air, fire, water (see **Vila:** *Shape-shifting the Elements,* pp. 174–177). Call in whatever you need or want to call in—power animal(s), the Goddess and the God, the Great Mystery, Grandmother Moon. Once you have cast the circle and called in what/whoever you choose you are ready to call in **Maat**. You may want to put the card representing **Maat** in the center of the circle or include something that represents **Maat** to you. It is best when you are calling in a Goddess to use your own words and speak directly from your heart. It is not the words you use that matter, it is the intent, coming sincerely and directly from the heart. Close your eyes and call her in with drumming, chanting, dancing, singing, with words spoken out loud or in silence. Open to her and sense, see, or feel her presence. Now hand over to her what requires justice in your life. Feel the situation being lifted off your shoulders. Really sense, see, or feel that **Maat** is going to take care of it. It is out of your life, off your back, removed from your mind. Thank **Maat** for coming and release her with gratitude. Now release what you have called in. Allow yourself to feel, sense, or see the circle you have cast disappearing into the air. Welcome back!

MAEVE

RESPONSIBILITY

I am a Warrioress
a Warrioress of the Heart
I am Queen
of the domain of myself
I am able to respond
in all situations
from the knowledge of who I am
My actions are who I am

THE GODDESS ORACLE

My beliefs are who I am
All I do is who I am
That which is outside of me
stays outside of me
That which I choose to let in
I own and acknowledge
How can you be responsible
if you do not own all aspects of yourself?
How can you be accountable
without being Queen over your own domain?
How can you serve your consort, your children, your community
if you are unwilling to acknowledge and answer for yourself?

Mythology

Maeve (pronounced *mah've*), whose name means "intoxicating," was associated with Ireland and represented the land's sovereignty and its magical center, Tara. Over time she became diminished to **Maeve**, the Queen, who could outrun horses, confer with birds, and bring men into the heat of desire with a mere look. In the Irish epic the *Tain Bo Cuillaigne,* **Maeve** (spelled Medb or Mebhdh) argues with her king over who has the most wealth, since in Celtic custom the wealthier one of the partnership is the ruler. He won because he had a magical bull. She decided to steal a magical red bull for herself. After much battle and bloodshed, **Maeve** won the red bull. However, when the two bulls met, they ripped each other to shreds.

THE GODDESSES

Meaning of the Card

Maeve strides boldly into your life to challenge you with the task of taking responsibility for your life. It is time for you to become "queen of your domain" by becoming aware of, then accountable for, all that you do, all that you are, all that you believe.

Are there places within you that seem as uncertain as uncharted waters? Do you seem to live your life on "automatic" as if you've been programmed by someone else? Perhaps you have been drifting along in a particular situation, instead of finding out if this is the best place for you. Or you are not willing to own your pieces, to acknowledge what you have done to help create the situation or relationship you are now in.

Maeve is here to remind you that the way to wholeness is by taking responsibility for your life, whatever shape it is in. For only by taking responsibility, by acknowledging where you are, who you are, what you are, can you create something different.

Ritual Suggestion: Owning Dance

Choose a time when you can feel safe in your surroundings, when you will not be disturbed, when you can make noise. You may light a candle and/or burn incense, whatever is helpful for your process.

First make a list using a single piece of paper for each thing in your life: your job, your children (if any), your relationships with friends, lovers, relatives, et cetera. How much you want to do at this time is your choice. Next to each word you have written, write what you're feeling about it. For example, Job: legal secretary.

THE GODDESS ORACLE

Feeling: hate. Then go on to the next piece of paper, and so on until you are done.

Gather up your pieces of paper and go to a place where you have room to move. Choose music that gets you moving in whatever way is appropriate for you or use a rattle or drum. Create a circle in the middle of your space by walking it or drawing it on the floor, or placing objects in a circle.

When you are ready, start the music. Give yourself permission to play, to really get into it and have a good time. For the time being, remain outside the circle. Pick up your first piece of paper. Speak the words that are on the piece of paper, followed by the words: "This is mine," as often or as many times as you need to feel that you have owned it. You can accompany your words with stamping or jumping or whatever movement feels right to you. When you are done, put that piece of paper in the center of your circle and move on to the next piece of paper. When you have finished with that piece of paper, place it in the circle with the first piece of paper. When you have gone through all your pieces of paper, dance or step into the circle and pick up all the pieces of paper. While standing still or continuing to move/dance, say: "This is all mine" as many times as you need to. Allow yourself to breathe it in, to own all that is represented on paper as yours.

When you feel ready, step out of the circle and blow out the candle. Offer thanks to yourself, thanks to **Maeve**, thanks to your life. Remove or take apart the circle. Let yourself feel wholeness and power now that you have nourished yourself with responsibility.

MAYA
ILLUSION

What is it about me that's so hard
  to grasp?
I dance the universal energy
always moving
always active
You can never see me
as I am veiled
and that veil is a by-product
of what I do
who I am
Go deeper
Don't get caught in the
magnificence of my creativity
My creation is the illusion
behind which lies
the knowledge that
all matter is energy
and all energy is one

Mythology

The Hindus and Buddhists of India worshipped **Maya** (pronounced *my'ah*) as the "Material Universe," as "Mother of Creation," "Weaver of the Web of Life," and as illusion. She is the virgin or maid part of the three-part **Kali** (the three aspects being virgin, mother, and crone). **Maya** is also worshipped in Nepal, Tibet, Asia, and the Himalayas. Her special attributes are intelligence, creativity, water, and magic. Here she is depicted lifting the veils of earthly form to reveal the true nature of the universe.

Meaning of the Card

Maya moves subtly into your life to tell you to face your illusion. It is time to see what is so, what is true, what is real. Are you caught in a particular situation and can't seem to move because it is hard to see clearly? Were you dazzled by what a certain reality seemed to offer you and now discover nothing there? Have you been listening to the words people speak rather than what's behind the words? **Maya** says it is easy to get caught up in illusion. Wholeness is nurtured when you accept where you are and forgive yourself, become aware of the illusion, then consciously lift the veils to experience the reality. Seeing the reality behind the illusion is what brings you power.

Ritual Suggestion: Parting the Veils of Illusion

You will need a pen and paper. Find a time and place when and where you will not be disturbed. Sit or lie comfortably with your spine straight and close your eyes. Inhale slowly and exhale slowly. Focus on your breath, coming in and going out. When ready, sense, see, or feel your current situation shrouded in veils.

THE GODDESSES

As you ask the question "What is happening?", see, feel, or sense those veils parting. Now open your eyes and take your paper and pen. Name the situation you are in, then describe it clinically: just the facts.

When finished, put your pen down and close your eyes. Focus on your breath coming in and going out. When ready, ask the second question: "How do I feel about the current situation?" and see, feel, or sense more veils lifting. Now open your eyes and write how you feel about the situation you are in. (If you need to get in touch with your feelings, see **Demeter:** *Feelings/ Emotions,* pp. 53–56.)

When finished, put down your pen and close your eyes. Focus on your breath. When ready, ask the third question: "What do I need?" and see, feel, or sense all the remaining veils dropping from your situation. Now open your eyes and write what you need.

Look down at your lists, the three threads entwined in the current situation. Ask yourself the question: "Does this situation serve me?" Write your answer. Focus again on your breath. See, feel, or sense your current situation for what it truly is. Stay in the place of the observer, rather than letting emotion cloud your perspective. Allow yourself to take in the clarity you feel. You have seen what is so and this brings power. Breathe in the power of clarity and vision that comes in viewing reality. Welcome back!

MINERVA

BELIEFS

I am what I think
my life is shaped and formed
by what I tell myself
Who I am in the world
is who I think I am
What I have in the world
is what I think I can have
The contents of my mind
are what I choose
I discard, cut out, drop
that which doesn't contribute
What others believe about me
is their story
It tells more about what they think
than who I am
In my journey
I make sure that what I carry
is of my own careful choosing
and serves me well

Mythology

Minerva (pronounced *mi-ner'vah*), the Roman and Etruscan Goddess of intelligence, creativity, wisdom, domestic skills, and handicrafts was the patroness of artisans, of all people whose handiwork was guided by their minds. Her very name comes from the ancient root for "mind." **Minerva** appears here with her sacred tree, the olive. She wears an aegis, which is a breastplate edged with snakes, and an owl on her headdress which identifies her as a Goddess of death and the deepest mysteries.

Meaning of the Card

Minerva has come to tell you it is time to examine your beliefs and change them if they do not nurture your wholeness. How are old, outworn, unhealthy thoughts undermining your life, your energy, your happiness? Do you believe what other people think and/or say about you? Are you still running the tape of negative messages your parents or caregivers gave you when you were a child? Do you believe the worst about yourself, or the best? Are your beliefs too rigid to permit and support your evolution? We all are born with a story. It is our choice whether we want to live the story we were born with or create one that nourishes all we want to be. **Minerva** says that wholeness is nurtured when you see yourself with all your parts—both dark and light—and choose your beliefs to serve your highest good.

Ritual Suggestion: What's in My Attic?

Find a time and a place where and when you will not be disturbed. You will need paper and a pen. Sit or lie comfortably with your spine straight and close your eyes. Take a deep breath, breathing into all the parts of your body, letting the breath fill you as if you were a balloon. When you are absolutely filled, release it. Take another deep breath and release it. Close your eyes and sense, feel, or see a flight of stairs leading up to an attic. It can be an attic you know well or one you imagine. Climb those stairs. At the top of the stairs is a door. You have the key to the door on a cord around your neck. Take the key and open the door. You enter a room. On one wall are shelves. On one of the shelves is a box marked "beliefs." Take the box down and open it. Inside the box are your beliefs. Reach inside, pull one out, and examine it. After you have finished examining it to your satisfaction, ask yourself the question: "Does this belief serve my highest good/wholeness?" If you answer yes, put it back into the box and take out another. If you answer no, then change the belief into something that serves you, something that feels good, something nurturing.

Repeat your new belief several times and feel it sinking into your heart, into your consciousness. Let yourself feel the joy of having this new belief. When finished, put the new and improved belief back into the box and return the box to the shelf. Close the attic door and lock it with your key. Come down the stairs. When you arrive at the foot of the stairs, take a deep breath and exhale slowly as you come back into your body. When you feel ready, open your eyes. Welcome back!

Note: If you find that your belief seems to resist your efforts to change it, repeat this ritual at another time. This is a process and the beliefs you are working with have been in place for a long time. Commitment is important here. You might even try writing your new belief and posting it in a prominent place where you will see it often.

MORGAN LE FAYE

RHYTHMS

When I dance with Life
I dance my own rhythm
I keep my own time
My soul's tides are aligned
and flow
with my beat: my own unique expression
By honoring myself
I honor all
When you dance with Life
what's your rhythm
Is it quick or slow
lively or liturgical
repetitious or ever-changing
Do you let the tempo serve you
or unnerve you
soothe you
or seethe you
mettle you
or unsettle you
Do you know?

Mythology

Morgan le Faye is a Celtic triple Goddess of death and rebirth, appearing as a beautiful young maiden, a powerful mother/creator, or a death-giving hag. She was also a sea Goddess, for her name

"Mor" in Celtic means sea. Her last name has two meanings: "the fairy" and "the fate." In the Arthurian legends, she was half-sister to Arthur. It is said she manipulated Mordred, **Morgan** and Arthur's son, by getting him to kill his father. As Arthur dies, **Morgan le Faye** comes to his aid by spiriting him to the magical island of Avalon, where she heals him, then casts him into a deep sleep from which he will awaken when the time is ripe.

Meaning of the Card

Morgan le Faye has come dancing into your life with her drums and her magic to invite you to discover and live your rhythms. What are your personal rhythms? Do you know the best time for you to exercise, sleep, eat, be creative, make love, work, et cetera? Or do you spend all your vitality adjusting to the rhythms imposed on you by your work, family, lover, friends? Have you been submerged in the life of another and lived his/her rhythms instead of your own? Perhaps you never discovered your own rhythms because you wanted to please those around you and be "one of the team." It is vital for you to live according to your own rhythms. Flowing with your rhythm brings you greater energy because you are no longer suppressing what is natural to you. **Morgan le Faye** says vitality, health, and wholeness are nurtured when you flow with your own unique beat rather than against it.

Ritual Suggestion: Journey to Avalon

Find a time and a place when and where you will not be disturbed. Sit or lie comfortably with your spine straight and close your eyes. Take a deep breath and release it slowly. Take another deep breath and release it as if you were a fire-breathing dragon, exhaling

THE GODDESSES

flames of tension. Take another deep breath and, as you release it, see how far you can exhale your flames of tension. Now take a deep breath and, as you exhale, see, sense, or feel that you are on a small boat. It can be a boat you are familiar with or one that exists in your imagination. The boat rocks back and forth, back and forth, and you are rocking into a deep state of relaxation with it. It feels so comfortable to be gently rocked by the boat as you are carried across the water, securely and safely.

You look up and see a curtain of mists. Slowly the mists open, creating a passageway for your boat. After you enter, the mists close. Before you is the island of Avalon. Your boat lands and you step out. **Morgan le Faye** greets you and welcomes you to Avalon.

She asks you what you need and you tell her you have come for assistance with your rhythms. She takes you by the hand and leads you to her magical scrying pond, in the middle of a circle of apple trees. You both sit on some low rocks at the edge of the pond. **Morgan le Faye** takes her wand and stirs the pond. When the pond becomes still again, what you see on the surface of the pond is exactly what you need. You thank **Morgan le Faye** for her help and she asks you for something. You give it to her in gratitude, with an open heart. Then she escorts you back to your boat.

You enter the boat and it takes off. Again, the mists part for you, then close. The gentle rocking of the boat is soothing. You are returning, feeling clear and centered; returning, feeling you know what you need to do; returning, feeling refreshed and revitalized.

You take a deep breath and release it slowly, coming fully back into your body. Take another deep breath and, as you release it, open your eyes. Welcome back!

NU KUA

ORDER

There is a Way
and I am that Way
the Way of Nature that moves in
    all things
In the beginning
I created the universal pattern
the Way things are
the Way things flow
the Way things need to be
Then
I sequenced the seasons
harmonized the hillsides
organized the oceans
till all was auspiciously arranged
I am the natural order of things
I am the Way

Mythology

At the time of what the Hopei and Shansi people of northern China call the Great Chaos in the universe, **Nu Kua** (pronounced *noo'kwah*), the dragon-bodied Goddess, came to restore order. She replaced the pillars of heaven with the legs of the great turtle and repaired the sky with colored stones. Her repairs enabled the rains to fall when needed and the seasons to come in their rightful order.

THE GODDESSES

The dragons on her two pillars guard the path of the sun and the moon. The compass she wears at her waist symbolizes order.

Meaning of the Card

Nu Kua floats into your life to assist you in creating order. Is chaos constantly peering around the edges of your life, threatening to overwhelm you if you relax for an instant? Have you let things pile up and bury you? Do you find you are excellent at organizing your boss, your family, your mate, but not yourself? Are you afraid of order, afraid that if you find a workable system for yourself you will feel locked in, unable to flow? Or perhaps you have created order in your life, but in a way that is stifling and stiff, solid, heavy, engraved in stone. Now is the time to nurture yourself with order that assists rather than chokes your life force. **Nu Kua** says that when life is ordered in the natural way, you nurture your path to wholeness. When you forcibly impose something unnatural from without, you create rebellion and resistance.

Ritual Suggestion: Journey to Nu Kua

Find a time and a place when and where you will not be disturbed. Sit or lie comfortably with your spine straight and close your eyes. Take a deep breath and release it slowly. Take another deep breath and, as you release it, feel yourself becoming lighter. Take another deep breath and, as you release it, feel yourself floating up, up, up. Up, up, up, feeling relaxed and at ease, feeling comfortable and safe. Up, up, up, floating deliciously and weightlessly, until you reach the palace of **Nu Kua**. The main gate opens for you. You walk through a series of doors which open for you till you are in the great throne room standing before **Nu Kua**.

She invites you to sit down and a chair is brought for you. She asks you what you need and you tell her you need her help creating order in your life. She asks you for a picture of the disorder in your life and you give it to her. She asks you questions about your disorder and you answer her. Then she tells you what you need to do. She asks you for a gift and you give it to her with an open heart. You thank her and return to the main gate through the doors, which close after you. At the main gate a fluffy white cloud approaches you and you lie on it. It takes you down, down, down; you feel clear and focused. Down, down, down, feeling refreshed and relaxed. Down, down, down, till you arrive back in your body. Take a deep breath and, as you release it, open your eyes. Welcome back!

NUT

MYSTERY

Reach for me
touch me
I am always beyond your grasp
Don't try to figure me out
for you can't
I am the ever-present unfathomable unknown
I am the immensity of the star-filled sky
I am beyond human comprehension

THE GODDESSES

In the vastness of my being
I am a mystery
even to myself

Mythology

Nut (pronounced *noot*) is the Egyptian Goddess of the night sky, also known as the Great Deep, the Celestial Vault, who daily gives birth to the sun each morning then consumes it again each night. Disapproving of the incest of **Nut** as she lay over her brother Geb, the earth, Ra, the sun or high God, had them pried apart. **Nut** was then lifted into the sky where she remains, her body formed into an arch. Painted inside the inner lid of a sarcophagus, she mothers and protects the dead on their journey.

Meaning of the Card

Nut's twinkling vast dark vault stretches out in your life to remind you to open to the mystery. Have you been planning every aspect of your life and left no room for mystery? Is your life wound up too tight? Are you trying to make everything safe by defining it, labeling it, knowing it all? Give way to the mystery, the unknowable. The Wise Woman knows there is much in the universe that will remain a mystery and leaves space for it in the weaving of her life. **Nut** says the way to nurture wholeness is for you to trust that the mystery you let in will be exactly what you need for your journey to wholeness.

Ritual Suggestion: Nut's Embrace

You can do this as a journey in imagination or as a ritual if you live where you feel safe outside at night. If you choose to journey, find a time and a place when and where you will not be disturbed. Sit or lie comfortably with your spine straight and close your eyes. Take a deep breath and exhale quickly. Take another deep breath and exhale slowly. Take another deep breath and exhale with the slowness of a turtle.

If you choose to enact this ritual, go outside. If you are journeying, visualize, sense, or feel the immensity of Nut's body, the night sky, above you. See her form clearly. She is smiling at you. She holds her hand out to you, inviting you to come to her. She points to a spiraling path of stars that begin to twinkle in front of you. You step onto the path of stars. Now you are surrounded by Nut's immensity, her vastness, her blackness. You see her waiting and you continue to climb the spiral path of stars until you are standing before her. She holds out her arms and you walk into her embrace. She holds you, and though you feel the warmth of her embrace, you also feel something you will never comprehend: her mystery. She urges you to open your heart to her and to trust her. You open your heart and experience a deep sense of oneness with the unknown. You feel safe and calm, centered and secure. You stay in her embrace until you feel full, satisfied, ready to move on. You thank Nut, and she tells you it is time to return. You walk the spiral path of stars back to Earth, back to your home, back to your body. Take a deep breath and, when ready, open your eyes. Welcome home!

THE GODDESSES

OSHUN

SENSUALITY

Oh let me delight you with beauty
so the eye may dance with joy
let me seduce you with scents
so that your nose inhales pleasure
let me tantalize your taste
till your tongue quivers
let me caress you with sound
that makes your ears sing and sing
let me touch your body
with waterfall music
and adorn your beauty with
golden bracelets and honey and perfume
and when all is experienced
when all your senses have been given play
when your spirit from the stars connects in a blissful way
with your body from the earth
then you will know sensuality

Mythology

Oshun (pronounced *oh-shun'*), the Brazilian Macumba Goddess of the waters—rivers, streams, brooks—is known for her love of beautiful things. She loves to adorn herself, especially in yellows and golds. Her rites at watery places include honoring her with honey and pennies (copper). Her necklace of cowrie shells symbolizes her knowledge and power in divination. It is said that the women dedicated to **Oshun** carry the special gift of their Goddess. They walk and dance in the most tantalizing and provocative ways. In their walk is the flow of the river. None can escape their charms.

Meaning of the Card

Oshun appears seductively in your life and cajoles you into remembering and honoring your sensuality. Wholeness is nourished by focusing your attention and time on your body, respecting and giving play to your senses and your sensuality. **Oshun** is here to tell you that it is time for sensuality. She invites you to follow her lead.

Ritual Suggestion: The Bath

Run a bath when you have time to give to yourself. Select some soothing music. Light a candle in the bathroom, so that the light is soft and gentle. When you are ready to enter the bath, add some essential oil(s) to the water so that you are enveloped in fragrance.

Let yourself surrender to the warmth of the water, feeling the wet heat seek out all the tense places in your body and replace them with warmth, relaxation, and openness. Let yourself drift in the water, basking in the heat, the fragrance, the music. Close your eyes and take a deep breath. Allow yourself to feel pleasure, to feel ease, to feel gratitude for the gift of your body and your senses. Stay in this state of relaxation for as long as feels right. Fifteen minutes is a good amount of time. When you are done with the bath, anoint your body with a natural body oil. Blow out your candle giving thanks to **Oshun**.

Oya
CHANGE

I work in ways deep
ever present
always moving
I work in ways dramatic
with thunder and lightning
sweeping and uprooting
I work in ways subtle
pushing and prodding
wearing and tearing
I swirl you and twirl you
I splatter you and scatter you
I shock you and rock you
I clear the way for what is to come
I can be slight or stupendous
brief or long lasting
uproaring or uprising
What I can't be is ignored

Mythology

In Africa, **Oya** (pronounced *oh-yah*) is the Yoruban Goddess of weather, especially tornadoes, lightning, destructive rainstorms, fire, female leadership, persuasive charm, and transformation. She is also one of the most powerful of Brazilian Macumba deities. When women find themselves in hard-to-resolve conflicts, she is the one to call on for protection. Wearing wine, her favorite color, and exhibiting nine whirlwinds (nine being her sacred number), she is depicted here with a turban twisted to appear like buffalo horns, for it is said she assumed the shape of a buffalo when wedded to Ogun.

Meaning of the Card

Oya storms into your life to tell you that change is calling, beckoning, and camping out on your doorstep. The way to wholeness for you lies in embracing change. Have you been too busy, too stressed, to attend to the changes needed in your life to nurture yourself? Is change so fearful a concept that you push it aside, play hide-and-seek with it, or just ignore it? Have you arranged your life so perfectly that there is no room left for potential? Time for change. Time to sweep out, sweep up, and be swept away. Perhaps you are in the midst of the Change (menopause) and are having trouble accepting it. Resistance to change brings more persistent change. Choosing to dance with change means you will flow with it. Let yourself be unsettled, prepare yourself for growth. Enter deeply into change's chaotic dance and you'll be richly blessed with abundant possibility. It is time for something completely different. Oya says that the earth must be dug up before anything can be planted and that change always brings you what you need on your path to wholeness.

Ritual Suggestion: Enlisting Change as Your Ally

Find a time and a place when and where you will not be disturbed. Sit or lie comfortably with your spine straight and close your eyes. Take a deep breath and release it slowly. Take another deep breath and this time release it while making the sounds of the wind. Take another deep breath and, as you release it, see, sense, or feel yourself walking along a path. The day is beautiful, perfect for a walk. The path takes you up and the path takes you down. You follow the path, surrendering to where it leads you, feeling more and more relaxed, more and more at ease.

Now the path begins to climb steadily. Up, up, up you go. Soon you have to climb hand over hand. Still the path climbs upward. You finally pull yourself onto an immense plateau. You have arrived on the Plain of Vision where the winds blow cool, clear, and clean. Here you can see clearly what you need to see.

Allow yourself to experience the swirling of the winds as your vision clears. You call **Oya** and she comes. She scoops you up in a powerful embrace. She asks you why you have come. You ask her, "What can I do to enlist change as my ally?" and she answers. Envision the answer clearly in your mind, then thank **Oya** for her help. She asks you for a gift and you give it to her with gratitude and an open heart. **Oya** embraces you again and vanishes.

Now it is time to return. You climb down slowly and carefully. Down, down, down, feeling calm and refreshed. Down, down, down, feeling at ease and centered till you are once more on the path. The path takes you through and the path takes you around. You follow, feeling a sense of peace. The path takes you down and the path takes you up, as you feel more and more awake. Take a deep breath and, as you release it slowly, come back into your body. Take another deep breath and open your eyes. Welcome back!

PACHAMAMA

HEALING/WHOLING/HOLY

I sing a song of love
from the stones of my body
from the high peaks of my mountains
from the hot sands of my deserts
I caress you with green leaves
green plants
green grasses
I bathe you in greenery
and feed you from my breast
the earth
I soothe you with sparkling waters
refresh you in my oceans
My song of love for you
is my body
the earth
there to feed you
clothe you
home you
Learn my song
and it will heal you
sing my song and it will whole you
dance with me and you'll be holy

THE GODDESSES

Mythology

To the pre-Incan peoples of Peru and Bolivia, **Pachamama** (pronounced *pah'cha-ma-ma*), or Mamapacha, is the Earth, worshipped in her many forms: the tilled fields, her mountains seen as breasts, the flowing rivers as her milk. To ensure good harvests, corn meal is sprinkled at planting and rituals celebrating her are performed. When the people fail to honor her, this dragon Goddess sends earthquakes as a reminder.

Meaning of the Card

Pachamama waits for you with open arms. It is time to open to **Pachamama**'s embrace. Now is the time to heal/whole and remember your holiness, remember yourself as a sacred being. Do you feel a connection with Earth Mother as a living entity or do you consider the earth an inert rock beneath your feet? Are you in the middle of some emotional pain that nothing seems to ease? Do you eat food and drink water without giving thanks to the earth? Are you looking for answers to questions? Do you spend time in nature opening to the earth and her vital energies? Opening to **Pachamama** can occur anyplace. You can commune with her in a city park, your own backyard, some remote forest, jungle, or desert. **Pachamama** says that healing/wholing is nurtured when you open to her.

Ritual Suggestion: Opening to Pachamama

If you can go out into nature and find a place where you feel safe, do so. Sit, stand, or lie comfortably on **Pachamama** with your spine straight. If this is not possible, find a time and a place indoors where and when you will not be disturbed. Sit or lie comfortably with your spine straight. Take a deep breath and inhale **Pachamama**'s fragrance. Do you smell her leaves, plants, or flowers? the dry smell of the desert or the bracing scent of the ocean? Take another deep breath and, as you release it, open to **Pachamama**. Let her surround you with her smells, her sensations. Let yourself feel enveloped by her in a loving, nurturing way. **Pachamama** is mother to all the creatures that walk on her and inhabit her. Let her healing ways comfort you, let her reweave any rips in the fabric of your being. You may see her standing in front of you, sitting next to you, or holding you with her arms. Be with **Pachamama** in whatever way is appropriate for you. Allow yourself to stay open until you feel filled, satiated by her. With an open heart give her whatever she asks for with gratitude. Take a deep breath and release it slowly. When you are ready, open your eyes. Know that you and **Pachamama** are connected. Welcome back!

PELE

AWAKENING

I surge I pulse I throb
I am never still
I am perpetual vibration
a rhythmic beat
the constant hum that you hear
I am always moving
way down in the deeps

THE GODDESSES

with fiery vitality
in places you can only feel
When necessary
with dramatic, fierce, volcanic eruptions
I wake you up
With lava and fire
I say "pay attention"

Mythology

Pele (pronounced *pay'lay*) is the volcano Goddess of the Polynesian peoples of Hawaii. According to legend she appears to people as a beautiful and mysterious young woman just before her volcano is about to erupt or as a gnarled old woman who lights her cigarette with the snap of her fingers. Although her priestesses, the queens of Hawaii, were converted to Christianity when Mauna Loa erupted in 1880, Princess Keelikolani recited the old chants, gave offerings of silk cloth, and poured brandy into the bubbling lava. **Pele**, thus appeased, grew calm.

Meaning of the Card

Pele's appearance signals a need for awakening. Have you been sitting still for too long? Have you been lulled into sleep by the evenness in your life? Has reality been too slippery to grasp? Get ready to awaken your awareness and come into full consciousness. Now is the time to see things as they really are, to initiate change so things can be as you want them to be. Now is the time to wake up to your potential and power, to move and shake. Pay attention to all that life is telling you. **Pele** says that when you nurture awakening, your life becomes creative rather than reactive —an infinitely more powerful place to be!

Ritual Suggestion: The Volcano

Choose a time and place when and where you will not be disturbed. Sit or lie comfortably. Close your eyes. Take a deep breath and release it, letting go of all that needs to be let go. Take another deep breath and see a volcano. It can be a volcano you know or one you invent. Let yourself see it, feel it, sense it, smell it. Now let your body become the volcano. How does it feel? Feel yourself connected to the core of the Earth. Feel the fire, the molten energy at the core of the Earth, vibrating, moving, humming. The molten energy begins to move and expand. First it enters your feet. Feel the liquid warmth. Then it moves into your legs, expanding and radiating energy, vitality, and pleasure. Then it moves into your torso where it connects with your spine.

The warmth moves slowly up your spine like liquid gold, caressing, relaxing, energizing. It feels deeply pleasurable. As it moves into your solar plexus (right above your navel), it radiates out to the rest of your body, down your arms, into your hands, out your fingertips.

Now it begins to climb upwards spreading vitality throughout your body. It moves up your spine to the top of your head where it erupts and pours down the surface of your skin, energizing and renewing, warming and revitalizing. You feel aware and awake, centered and relaxed, ready for anything. Welcome back!

RHIANNON

DOUBT

I wasn't certain
after all, my face had blood on it
all fingers pointed to me
could I have killed him
my infant son
my own
in my sleep
I was accused
and found guilty
and I doubted myself
for seven long years
I played horse to my lord husband Pwyll's guests
carrying them into court
carrying them out again
and the times were many when I doubted myself
doubted along with all the other humans
that because I was from the Other World
anything was possible

Mythology

The Welsh horse Goddess of the Underworld—Rigatona, or Great Queen—was **Rhiannon**'s (pronounced *ree-ah'nin*) original name. Her story was reduced to something of a fairytale, just as her name was changed from Great Queen. Though not human, she married

Pwyll, a mortal, and bore him a son who disappeared at birth. The attendant maids smeared the blood of a puppy on **Rhiannon's** face and accused her of eating her child. **Rhiannon** was sentenced to carry all her husband's guests on her back. When her son reappeared after seven years, all lived happily ever after.

Meaning of the Card

Rhiannon gallops into your life to tell you how to work with doubt. To doubt someone or something when your instincts are giving you warning signals is healthy. To spend time doubting yourself is self-negating and not very helpful. The best way of working with self-doubt is to turn it into self-questioning. Self-doubt leads you nowhere. Self-questioning gives you answers. Do you get stuck in doubt and let it turn your optimism into despair, your confidence into low self-esteem, your vitality into sluggishness and procrastination? Does doubt align itself with your fears to keep you from succeeding? Do the doubts of others shipwreck your dreamboat? Perhaps where the outside world is concerned you need to exercise a bit more skepticism, rather than trusting blindly. **Rhiannon** tells you not to let doubt erode your sacred self. Allow yourself to question rather than doubt so that you can gain the answers you need to continue on your path to wholeness.

Ritual Suggestion: Doubt Alchemy

Find a time and a place when and where you will not be disturbed. Sit or lie comfortably with your spine straight and close your eyes. Take a deep breath and release it slowly. Take another deep breath and exhale all your stress and tension through your nose, as if you

THE GODDESSES

were a whale spouting water. Take another deep breath and, as you release it see, sense, or feel a tree. It can be a tree you are familiar with or one that exists only in your imagination. Take a deep breath and, as you release it, stand in front of the tree. Reach out and feel the bark of the tree. What do the leaves look like? Now allow your body to turn to water and let yourself rain into the earth. Feel yourself being absorbed into the roots of your tree.

Now you are traveling down, down, down, deeper and deeper and deeper. It feels safe and comfortable, warm and cozy, as you go down, down, down. Feeling more and more relaxed as you go deeper and deeper and deeper. You see a rider on a white horse. It is **Rhiannon** and you ask her to stop. She stops, dismounts, and walks up to you. You tell her you need her help to transform your doubts and she agrees to help you. You tell her your first doubt and she puts it into the form of a question. You answer the question, then tell her your second doubt and so on until you have given **Rhiannon** all your doubts and she has transformed them all into questions, which you have answered. You thank her for her help and she asks you for a gift. You give her what she asks for with an open heart. **Rhiannon** then mounts her horse and gallops away as you return to the tree root.

Entering the root you travel up, up, up, feeling confident, secure, and clear. Up, up, up, feeling energized, refreshed, balanced. You reach the trunk of the tree and pop out of a branch, landing on the ground in front of the tree. Take a deep breath and, as you exhale, come back into your body. Take another deep breath and, as you exhale, open your eyes. Welcome back!

SEDNA

VICTIM

My fingers were cut off then
I was kicked
I was hurt
I was wounded
I was lied to
I was betrayed
I was abandoned
My suffering was great
but down below in the deeps
in the heart of the ocean
where I was left to die
I realized my powerlessness
the way my life was lived
helpless and afraid
always being done to
instead of doing
and saw what I did
As realization expanded my consciousness
fish and sea mammals
grew out of my cut fingers
I became "old food dish"
She who provided for her people
Victim no more

THE GODDESSES

Mythology

The Inuit of North America call their sea Goddess **Sedna** (pronounced *sed'nah*). **Sedna** was once a beautiful woman who was not satisfied with the many suitors who courted her. Wooed by a seagull with promises of plenty of food and servants, she went to live with the bird people. Instead of the promised conditions, she was forced to live in filth and squalor. When her father came for a visit, she begged him to take her back home with him across the waters. The bird people pursued them and to save his life, her father threw **Sedna** overboard. When she tried to climb back into the boat, he cut off her fingers. **Sedna's** cut fingers transformed into fish and sea mammals.

Meaning of the Card

Sedna swims into your life to tell you to stop being a victim. The way to wholeness is to recognize how you've been caught up in and are living the victim archetype, then to change the pattern by empowering yourself. Are you fond of saying, "Why is this happening to me?" Don't get stuck in the "why." Look realistically at what you are creating, then work to change it. Do you feel your needs are too insignificant to negotiate? Does everyone in your life seem to take advantage of you? Your way to wholeness lies in recognizing when you are playing the victim and stopping it. **Sedna** says we have all been victimized by something, by patriarchal institutions, discrimination based on race, gender, sexual preference, religion, or color. She encourages you to claim your power (see **Lilith**: *Power,* pp. 106–110). **Sedna** says you are too precious and necessary in this dance of life to waste valuable energy and time being a victim. Rather than dissipating your energy, create what you want.

Ritual Suggestion: Dancing Your Victim

Find a time and a place when and where you will not be disturbed. Select music to dance to or make your own music with a drum or rattle. Allow yourself space to move around; if you prefer, you can do this as a visual journey.

Place **Sedna**'s card where she can witness your dance. You can even speak directly to her and ask her to be present. Breathe deeply and relax. When you feel ready, turn on your music and/or take up your rattle or drum. Begin by stating out loud "I am a victim." Keep stating it over and over. Allow that chant to take you where you need to go. Your chant could lead to other phrases or shouts or cries. Let whatever needs to come up, come up. Let your body express your feelings in movement. You can do something as simple as stamping your feet or jumping up and down. Let all be expressed that needs to be expressed and keep the dance going until you are finished.

Now chant the words "I am powerful," and accompany your chant with movements till you feel powerful, strong, and secure. Take a deep breath and release it slowly. Give thanks to **Sedna** for her assistance. Welcome, woman of power!

SEKHMET

ANGER AND RAGE

I burn and fume
and shoot daggers from my eyes
I erupt and roar
(though you've not pulled my tail)
my edges are sharp
and I cut deep
my energy is strong and fierce
and my displeasure
needs to be expressed
Though sometimes mild
I can be very intense
Once incited
I am difficult to put out
I am always appropriate
always needed
Don't try to get rid of me
I need to be acknowledged and heard
I am anger

Mythology

Sekhmet (pronounced *sek'met*), the lion-headed Egyptian Sun Goddess, is known as the destructive aspect of the Sun. Vowing to destroy all humanity in a fit of rage, she went on a killing spree. She was stopped by the intervention of Ra, the high God, who put huge vats of beer mixed with pomegranate juice in her path.

Mistaking it for human blood, **Sekhmet** consumed the drink and became intoxicated. When she woke up, her rage was gone. Red in this painting signifies **Sekhmet**'s scorching, smoldering nature.

Meaning of the Card

Sekhmet leaps into your life to help you face your anger. Does anger, yours or someone else's, make you feel uncomfortable? Do you fear your anger because you were taught anger isn't nice? or that expressing anger is ugly? Have you repressed or disconnected from it so much so that you don't know how to express it now? Perhaps you've gone beyond anger to rage. Rage is accumulated anger gone out of control. Perhaps you're in a slow boil all the time and don't know how to take the pot from the fire. **Sekhmet** says our anger is part of our power as women. Don't give away your anger. Learn to express it in a way that it can be heard. Learn to transform it so it empowers and energizes you. Your path to wholeness will be more vital when you make anger your ally.

Ritual Suggestion: Dancing with Sekhmet

Find a time and a place when and where you will not be disturbed and where you can make noise. You will need a drum or pillow or bataka bat.* You can dance or do this while sitting, whatever feels appropriate for you. Sit or lie comfortably with your spine straight. Take a deep breath and release it slowly on the count of eight. Take another deep breath and sense, visualize, or feel a beach. It can be a beach you know or one that you imagine. Take

---

*Bataka bat is a bat made of foam that is used to safely express anger and rage.

a slow deep breath, inhaling the smell of the sea and, as you release it, go there. Feel the hot sun on your skin and the cool breeze from the ocean. Call **Sekhmet** and ask her to be present to help you with and to witness your anger. **Sekhmet** appears and sits in front of you.

Ask yourself, "Where do I have anger?" and listen for the answer. (It can be a recent anger or a long-buried one.) **Sekhmet** tells you to search for your anger in a relaxed way and assures you that if you call, it will come. When you have it, allow yourself to relive the incident in which you felt anger, while repeating the words "I am angry." Also say what you are angry about. **Sekhmet** witnesses your anger and says, "I hear you are angry."

From your safe space on the beach, either sit or stand, but keep repeating the words, "I am angry." If you have a drum, beat your feelings of anger on the drum. If you choose to beat a pillow or bataka bat, allow your body to feel the anger and express it. Move, vocalize, dance, or do whatever is appropriate. Above all, allow yourself to feel your anger and express it. Know that it is safe to do so, that **Sekhmet** is witnessing your anger and loving you for it, that it is yours and you have a right to it. Press deeper into the anger until you feel done or until it changes into something else.

When you are finished, take a deep breath, inhale all the energy you have raised and transformed. **Sekhmet** tells you what a joy it is to have witnessed and held the space for you to express your anger. You feel energized and refreshed. You thank **Sekhmet** and she asks you for a gift. You give it to her with an open heart, then she leaves. Take another deep breath and, as you release it, open your eyes. Welcome back!

SHAKTI

ENERGY

I am the ultimate source
dancing through all forms
I am the animating force
vibrating the world into being
I activate
invigorate
potentiate
Let me fill you
with cosmic ecstasy
Let me reconnect you
recharge you
renew you
I am the sweet-bliss honey nectar
that snakes up your spine
connecting all your chakras
into one big orgasmic orgy
of power
vitality
ENERGY!

Mythology

In Hindu India, **Shakti** (pronounced *shock'tee*), the Goddess, is active, powerful, vital—the animating force of the universe. The masculine is the passive, inert, dormant force. Each **Shakti** has her God with whom she unites in sexual union. Without union,

THE GODDESSES

neither can do anything. To the Tantric mystics, the ultimate union with **Shakti** happens at the moment of death. **Shakti**, portrayed here seated within the luminous world egg, is protected by the serpent, kundalini, the emanation of her own divine energy.

Meaning of the Card

Shakti explodes into your life to energize and vitalize you. The way to wholeness for you now lies in learning to work with **Shakti**: divine, cosmic, orgasmic Goddess energy. Have you been feeling tired? Do life and all its demands exhaust you? Do you keep giving your energy, your vitality, without taking in, recharging, revitalizing? Perhaps there is something you want to manifest but don't feel you have enough energy to do it. **Shakti** says there is abundant energy available for you. All you need to do is learn how to connect with it.

Ritual Suggestion: Cosmic Chakra Orgasm*

Find a time and a place where you will not be disturbed. Sit or lie comfortably with your spine straight and close your eyes. Take a deep breath and, as you release it slowly, feel yourself pulling your stress and tension off over your head, as if it were a tight-fitting dress. Toss it away, far from you.

Continue to breathe in a relaxed and even way. Picture, sense, or feel energy vibrating in the core of the earth. Imagine a long hose from your vulva, extending down into the earth. When you inhale, you open the valves on the hose and earth energy comes pulsing up. Draw that energy up into your first chakra in a way

---

* Chakras are energy centers. There are seven chakras located in the body.

THE GODDESS ORACLE

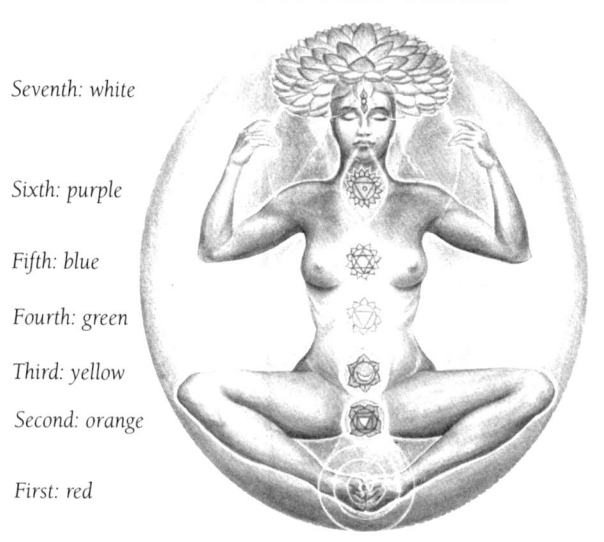

Seventh: white

Sixth: purple

Fifth: blue

Fourth: green

Third: yellow

Second: orange

First: red

Diagram of Chakras

that feels good. As the energy reaches your first chakra, it explodes into the color red, so that your first chakra is filled with spinning red energy. Take a moment to experience the feelings and sensations as your first chakra is filled with red vital energy. One sensation may be that you are sitting on a hose of continually flowing red energy that keeps pumping into your first chakra.

When ready, draw up the red energy from the first chakra to the second chakra where your womb is. Here the energy explodes filling your second chakra with vibrating, orange energy. Take time to experience the delicious sensations of having both your chakras filled with revitalizing energy.

Now draw the red energy up from the first chakra into the orange second chakra and up into the third chakra, which is

THE GODDESSES

located in your solar plexus. As the energy reaches your third chakra, it explodes into the color yellow, so that your third chakra is pulsing with electric yellow energy. Take time to enjoy having three chakras filled with invigorating energy.

Now feel the energy flowing up through each chakra to the fourth chakra, located in the middle of your chest roughly where your heart is. As the energy reaches your fourth chakra, it explodes into the color emerald green, so that your fourth chakra is filled with vibrant emerald green energy. Take time to feel the pleasurable sensations of having four chakras filled with vital energy.

Feel, sense, or see the energy moving through you to your fifth chakra at your throat. The energy reaching your throat fills your fifth chakra with electric blue energy. Take a moment to experience the pleasure of having five chakras filled with energy.

The energy oozes through you till it reaches your sixth chakra, the place between your eyebrows or your "third eye," where it explodes in the color purple. Allow yourself to feel the pulsing of energy in all six chakras.

The energy now slowly moves up through your chakras, building in intensity from the first, second, third, fourth, fifth, sixth, till it reaches the seventh chakra located at the crown of your head, where it explodes into white iridescent light. You feel powerfully charged with energy. All your chakras are crackling and vibrating with delicious, pleasurable energy. Stay with this for as long as is appropriate for you. Be sure to drink it into all your cells.

Now, see, sense, or feel the energy of the universe. Is it hot and fiery, like the sun? or silvery cool like moonbeams? or quiet and immense like the expansiveness of space? As you inhale, draw that energy into your seventh, or crown, chakra. Feel the earth energy and cosmic energy make love in your crown chakra, filling that chakra with the joy of union.

Allow the exquisiteness of the cosmic energy to pour down into the sixth chakra, gently filling and caressing, penetrating and blending with the earth energy, until you feel the sixth chakra explode with the union of earth and cosmos.

Now the energy from the cosmos slowly and sweetly moves into the fifth chakra, where it combines with the earth energy. The cosmic energy moves into your fourth, or heart, chakra. There it combines with the emerald green earth energy, until both are exploding in the passion of their union and you experience bliss. The cosmic energy is now pulled into the third chakra where it unites with the earth energy, until both are swirling, twirling, whirling, doing their dance of love, and you are feeling ecstasy. The cosmic energy pours into the second chakra. It meets the earth energy and both energies make love until you are rocked with bliss. When the cosmic energy enters the first chakra and unites with the earth energy, there is an orgasmic explosion. You feel ecstatic. All your chakras have experienced cosmic orgasm and you feel energized, relaxed, and totally refreshed.

When you feel filled, it is time to cover your chakras. Beginning with your seventh chakra, imagine a cap or lid being placed over the chakra to keep the energy inside you. After capping the seventh chakra, cap the sixth, then the fifth, fourth, third second, and first. Take a deep breath and open your eyes. Welcome back!

THE GODDESSES

SHEILA NA GIG

OPENING

I flash my vulva for all to see
I stretch it wide
the gateway that all comes through
the passageway to life
I say come through my doorway
open yourself to what is
if you have something important
show it
so everyone can see
I am the opening to this world
the sacred and the silly
the wild and the wooly
the bold and the brazen
I am the Hag
opened by so many turnings
broken down
broken in
broken through
I am the portal to Life
and I say
Open Up!

Mythology

Ancient Irish Goddess of birth and death, **Sheila Na Gig**'s (pronounced *shee'lah-nah-hig*) grinning figure with both hands holding open her yoni adorned many a church doorway, till she was torn down or smashed by the offended. The Celts honored the sacred power of woman's genitalia and used sculptures of such for protection. **Sheila Na Gig** is portrayed here as a hag (woman of wisdom) in all her glory: rib cage of bone, breasts dried out and sagging, with few remaining teeth and little hair, yet vibrant and defiant in the beauty of her age. This beauty is the right of all women to claim. She dares you to look at her, face your fears of aging, and triumph in your celebration of what will age and die.

Meaning of the Card

Sheila Na Gig grins at you provocatively and invites you to join her in opening. Now is the time to open to new experiences, people, places, and things. Now is the time to begin new projects, forge new directions, venture out boldly. The universe invites you to come out and play. Perhaps you've had to contract your energy to deal with a wounding, a grieving, an ending. Or you haven't felt it was safe to open up. You may have needed a time of seclusion, sorting out, and focusing inward. **Sheila Na Gig** is here to remind you that a period of contraction is followed by expansion and opening. It is time to nurture wholeness by integrating what the stretching, expanding, and opening will bring.

Ritual Suggestion: Creating Opening

Find a time and a place when and where you will not be disturbed. Sit or lie down with your spine straight. Close your eyes. Take a deep breath and release it with whatever sound you need to make. Take another deep breath and release it slowly with more sound. Let everything go into that sound that you do not need to carry.

THE GODDESSES

Beginning at your toes feel, sense, or visualize your body slowly turning a deeply relaxing green, the earth mother's own color. With each breath you take, you inhale green; with each breath you exhale, the green permeates and moves up your body till you are deeply relaxed and completely green.

Now see, sense, or feel a doorway in front of you. Is it ornate with a door of solid gold, or a simple but elegant wooden doorway? Is it wide or narrow, small or tall? Allow your doorway to suit your needs. When you are done creating the "doorway of your dreams," stand in front of it and admire your work.

Behind the door that you have just created lies the Otherworld. In the Otherworld is something you need to see and/or experience for your life right now. When you feel ready, open the door and walk into the Otherworld. Really feel yourself open as you open your door. When you are finished with what you need to see and/or experience in the Otherworld, come back through the doorway and close the door.

Take a look at your body and ask yourself: "Where do I need to open?" Then visualize, create, sense, and/or feel a doorway in yourself. Open the door and let in what is needed. Does your heart need to open to love? or your lungs to forgiveness? When you feel that you have gotten what you need, close the door.

Sense, feel, or see your body being green again. Take a deep breath; as you exhale, the green leaves your head. Take another deep breath; as you exhale, the green retreats from your shoulders, chest, and arms. Keep inhaling and exhaling until all the green is gone and you are totally present and refreshed, relaxed and energized. Welcome back!

SOPHIA

WISDOM

From the moment you enter
till the time you surrender to death
all that you experience
directly for yourself
all the burnt fingers
to discover the fire is hot
all the falling flat
when your reach exceeds your grasp
all the explorations
of territory known and unknown
all these are pathways to me
Seek to know
and you are me
stretch to become
and you are me
The Feminine quests for wisdom
The Feminine is part of all women
all women are the Goddess
all women have wisdom
all women are Sophia

Mythology

Sophia (pronounced *sew-fee'ah*) in Greek, Hohkma in Hebrew, Sapientia in Latin, all mean wisdom. The Judeo-Christian God's female soul, source of his true power, is **Sophia**. As Goddess of wisdom, her faces are many: Black Goddess, Divine Feminine, Mother of God. To the Gnostic Christians, **Sophia** was the Mother of Creation; her consort and assistant was Jehovah. Her sacred shrine, Hagia Sophia in Istanbul, is one of the seven wonders of the world. Her symbol, the dove, represents spirit; she is crowned by stars, a Middle Eastern icon, to indicate her absolute divinity.

Meaning of the Card

Pregnant **Sophia** holds out her cup of wisdom to you. It is time to connect with your own deep, enriching wisdom, time for stillness and introspection, time to listen to what needs to be heard. Perhaps you are in a situation where you need guidance. Perhaps you find yourself in similar situations over and over again. When you take the time to listen to your own inner **Sophia** you can get what you need.

Ritual Suggestion: Connecting with Your Inner Sophia

Find a time and a place when and where you will not be disturbed. Sit or lie comfortably with your spine straight and close your eyes. Take a deep breath and release it through the soles of your feet. Take another deep breath and, as you release it, feel all the tension being gently pulled out of your body, like a long thread, from the soles of your feet. Take another deep breath and, as you release it, allow yourself to relax deeply. Feel a sense of well-being spread like rose-colored warmth throughout your entire body.

Now find the place inside where your **Sophia** lives. Does she live on top of a mountain? beneath the sea in a palace? in a cave? a tree? the desert? Does she live in your heart? in your womb? in your head? Once you have an image, feeling, or sensation of where

THE GODDESS ORACLE

she is, go there. What are the smells of the place where your Sophia lives—the textures, the plants, the wildlife? Now that you have familiarized yourself with Sophia's surroundings, you are ready to meet her and she appears before you.

You ask Sophia what you need to ask her. She responds and you thank her. She asks you for a gift and you give it to her with an open heart. She tells you to come to her anytime, for she is always there within you. You are always welcome. She embraces you and gives you a kiss on your forehead. Your forehead tingles with delight as you take a deep breath and open your eyes. Welcome back!

SPHINX

CHALLENGE

If I ask the question that provokes
will you stretch to find the answer
Will you take up the gauntlet flung
boldly
and defiantly answer the call
Will you meet my challenge
with tingling in your blood
with your hair blowing electric in the wind
with all your being
knowing that every challenge
is an opportunity
every challenge

160

presents a gift
every challenge
is there to serve you
or not
It's your choice

Mythology

The **Sphinx** appears in Greek mythology as the monster—a woman's head and breasts, dog's body, lion's paws, wings of an eagle, and the tail of a serpent—who questioned Oedipus. To the ancient Egyptians, she symbolically represented the Nile and its seasons. She was also a manifestation of **Hathor**, Goddess of birth and death. The **Sphinx** of Egypt was built as guardian of the horizons, the rising and setting sun. It held the keys to the wisdom gates. In the path to deep knowing, initiates had to confront the challenges that the **Sphinx** posed.

Meaning of the Card

The **Sphinx** will not let you pass until you respond to her challenge. She asks: "How can you meet a challenge and prosper in all the aspects of your being?" You can let yourself get torn down by challenge, or kicked or pounded or defeated, but how can you take the challenge and use its energy to nurture yourself? Have you been running from challenges all your life and now find you haven't developed the energy or power to face them? Perhaps it's easier to ignore challenge and go on with self-limiting behavior. Or maybe you feel that life is all messed up. Whatever way you have been dancing with challenge in the past has to change.

THE GODDESS ORACLE

The greatest challenge in living is how you respond to challenges. The **Sphinx** says the only way to wholeness on your path is to meet your challenges face-to-face.

Ritual Suggestion: Meeting Challenge Face-to-Face

Find a time and a place when and where you will not be disturbed. Sit or lie comfortably with your back straight and close your eyes. Take a deep breath and release it slowly. Take another deep breath and release it with a sigh. Take another deep breath and release it, putting all your stress and tension into a hum. Take a final deep breath and envision, sense, or feel the steep incline of a hill before you. It could be one you have encountered before or one you imagine. There is a path on the incline and you begin walking up it. At first it rises gently, then gives way to flat land. Then it rises again, this time sharply, so you must climb, hand over hand and foot over foot till you reach a small cottage. You are out of breath and thirsty and decide to knock at the door of the cottage.

An old, very handsome Wise Woman opens the door. "I have been expecting you," she tells you. You ask for a drink of water and the Wise Woman takes you to the back of the cottage, hands you a mug, points to a sacred spring, and tells you to refresh yourself with its water. You dip your mug in the sacred spring and drink. The water quenches your thirst and leaves you feeling calm and refreshed.

Now the Wise Woman takes you by the hand and leads you into her cottage. The cottage is filled with wondrous and magical things, beautiful and delightful things. "I have something you need," she explains as she puts a large package in your hands. It

THE GODDESSES

is heavy. "Open the package when you arrive on the Plain of Vision. Now it is time for you to go." She escorts you to the door and hugs you. You thank her and leave.

The path takes you onto an enormous plateau. It is the Plain of Vision, where the winds blow cool, clear, and clean. Where you can see all that you need to see. Take a deep breath and inhale the clarity of the Plain of Vision.

You put the package on the ground and squat down to open it. Inside is a suit of chain mail and a sword. You put on the suit of mail. It fits perfectly. You grasp the sword, slashing the air. It feels good in your hand, the right weight and balance.

Something lands at your feet. You bend down to pick it up. It is a glove of mail, a gauntlet. A voice says, "Are you prepared to meet me?" You pick up the gauntlet and stand to face your challenge, who is masked, before you. You toss back the gauntlet, which is then put on by your challenge. Your swords cross and you begin the fight. Your challenge tries to trip you up, but you manage to breathe deeply and stay on your feet. Your challenge tries to divert your attention, but you manage to breathe deeply and stay focused. Your challenge is strong and persistent and tries to wear you out, but you stay centered and strong by breathing deeply, drawing up limitless energy from the earth into your body.

Finally your challenge tells you it will stop this fight if you will embrace it. You sheathe your sword and hold out your arms, and your challenge moves into them. As you both embrace, your suits of mail dissolve and your swords vanish. You hold each other with love and acceptance. Your challenge is transformed into light which is then absorbed into your body and becomes a part of you. You feel strengthened and revitalized.

You leave the Plain of Vision, going down the path. The cottage of the old Wise Woman is no longer there. You continue down the path feeling refreshed and whole, feeling energized and emancipated, feeling centered and steadied. When you reach the bottom of the incline, you take a deep breath and release it slowly, coming back fully into your body. Take another deep breath and release it slowly. When you feel ready, open your eyes. Welcome back!

SULIS

ILLNESS/WELLNESS

It is all one
being ill
being well
It is all energy
energy in constant motion
energy in constant flux
restless energy that is never still
ruthless energy that acts like a steam roller
boundless energy that brings possibilities
sparkling energy that tickles and sings
stored energy that waits for release
The healing waters at my shrine
regenerated

revitalized
brought clarity
mended holes
opened vision
allowed flow
With energy flowing
the dance of life resumes
illness and wellness
all one
all energy
all flow

Mythology

The ancient British called on and/or visited **Sulis** (pronounced *soo'lis*) at her spa-shrine in Bath for health and healing. Her waters there were said to be miraculous in their ability to affect cures. "Sul" is Celtic for "sun" and "eye" and she is thought to be a sun Goddess. Pictured here swimming up through her healing waters into the light of the sun, she represents the depths all people must plumb in their journey to light, health, and wholeness.

Meaning of the Card

Sulis has come to tell you that it is time to embrace the dance of illness/wellness. Make time for yourself and nourish the energy you have. It is time to let go of everything and make you a priority. It is time to ask for what you need and let it in. Give yourself permission to seek support and assistance for your healing process. Illness is our body's call for time off, time out, or just plain time. Illness is a way for us to come face-to-face with what is no longer working for us and change it. Have you been ignoring your own deep requests for more time, more space, more attention? Perhaps you've been too busy attending to everyone else's needs and putting your own last. Perhaps illness is the only way out of a messy or painful situation. Do you experience any resistance to being in the dance of illness/wellness? any blame? Regardless of what brought you to this dance, you are here and need to put everything aside that doesn't nourish and support your healing. The way to wholeness for you now lies in recognizing your own needs and putting them first, nourishing your energy, and allowing new ways of being with yourself that support health and vitality. **Sulis** says that the way you manage your energy can mean the difference between illness and wellness. Illness is the time to direct the flow of energy inward; wellness is the time for energy to be focused outward.

Ritual Suggestion: Recalling and Rebuilding Your Inner Fire

Find a time and place when and where you will not be disturbed. Sit or lie comfortably with your back straight and close your eyes. Take a deep breath and release it with a hum. Take another deep breath and release it with an "ahhhhh." Take a third deep breath and, as you release it, visualize a tree. It can be a tree you are familiar with or a tree you invent. Take another deep breath and stand in front of the tree. Feel the bark. Smell its tree scent. The more you can bring your senses into this journey, the deeper your experience will be.

There is a large opening in the trunk of the tree. You enter it and go down, down, down, deeper and deeper and deeper. The

THE GODDESSES

tree's root is comfortable and warm and you feel pleasantly relaxed. Continue going down, down, down, deeper and deeper and deeper until you see a faint light at the end. You reach the end of the root and step out onto a beautiful path made of shiny, colorful stones. Alongside the path are plants. As you walk the path of stones, you find yourself drawn to one particular plant. You stop and ask the plant its name. It tells you and says that it is your plant ally and will help you in your dance of illness/wellness. You thank the plant and continue along the path of stones.

The path takes you to a large temple, the Atlantian Healing Temple. You enter the temple. In the center is a large emerald healing slab, which you lie on. The stone conforms to your body's contours and temperature and is very comfortable.

Sulis appears and says she is here to assist you. She tells you that your body is composed of energy fibers and that you have over spent your energy by giving it to people, situations, outmoded thought forms that no longer serve you. It is now time for you to recall those energies that are sapping your vitality and keeping you from wellness.

As you listen to **Sulis**, you feel the energy fibers of your body as individual orange strands extending out from your womb into the world. You feel weight tugging at them, like an airborne kite on a windy day. As you take hold of one energy strand and begin to pull it in, your vitality begins to rise. You feel yourself reabsorbing the energy you have been giving away. Continue to do this until all your energy fibers are back and you have reabsorbed all your energy or until you feel you have done what is appropriate for you. When finished, you and **Sulis** leave the Atlantian Healing

Temple, again walking on the stone path, which now vibrates beneath your feet.

Sulis takes your hand and instantly you are transported to her shrine at Bath, England. She leads you slowly into her thermal healing waters and leaves you soaking in them while she continues walking into the waters until she merges with the water. Take in the deeply healing heat, her love for you. As you absorb the healing of the waters, your energy fibers begin to tingle and glow a deep orange. Remain in the waters for as long as is appropriate for you, then get out, feeling refreshed, recharged, and revitalized.

Return on the path of stones to the root of the tree. You enter the root and begin coming up, up, up, through the warmth and comfort of the root, up, up, up, into the tree feeling relaxed and strong, feeling awake, vital, whole. You step out of the tree. Take a deep breath and, as you slowly exhale, return to your body. Take another deep breath and when you exhale, if ready, open your eyes. Welcome back!

TARA

CENTERING

I sit with my attention focused on my breath
breathing in and out
inhaling and exhaling
taking in and letting go
the dance of creation
the dance of the universe
the dance of life

THE GODDESSES

I sit in stillness
in focused awareness
breathing in and out
as the ocean that is life
churns and pulses around me
as oceans of incarnations
swirl and twirl through me
beside me
all around me
My eyes see all
know all
and watch
As I breathe
Still. Focused. Aware. Centered.

Mythology

Tara (pronounced *tah'rah*), who originated in India and whose name means "star," is a major Goddess in the Tibetan pantheon. She is known to help those who call upon her in tumultuous times of need, to steer a clear path, to find the stillness and strength within. She is also the Goddess of self-mastery and mysticism. From the first tear of compassion, a lake was formed. From the middle of this lake, a lotus emerged. When it bloomed, **Tara** emerged. Although offered reincarnation in male form, she swore to be ever incarnated as a woman.

Meaning of the Card

Tara is here to remind you to center. It is time to nourish wholeness by going within and strengthening your center by focusing your awareness. Let the turmoil of life go on without you. It is hard to hear your own voice in the midst of the frenzy of life. Go into the quiet, go into the calm. When you return you will be stronger and more capable of dancing with what life has to offer.

Ritual Suggestion: Meeting Tara Through the Breath

Find a quiet time and place when and where you will not be disturbed. Sit or lie comfortably with your spine straight and close your eyes. Take a deep breath and let everything go. Shake out your body. Focus your awareness on your womb. How does she feel? Are you ovulating or bleeding? pre-menstrual? post-menopausal? Notice how your womb feels. Now take a deep breath inhaling into your womb, your center. Hold the breath there. Focus on the sensation. What does it feel like? When you feel ready, exhale from your womb. Feel the air exiting through your vagina and out through your labia.

Now you are ready to begin a count of inhalations, holdings, and exhalations, all from your womb, the center of your being. Close your eyes. Inhale into your womb for a count of six. Allow yourself to feel centered, focused, and alive. Hold the air in your womb for six counts as you feel the busyness of life moving away from your calm, focused center. Then exhale from your womb for six counts, letting go of whatever is no longer needed. Do this for a minimum of five minutes. If you wish, you can increase this. If you find six counts to be an easy and comfortable number, then increase to eight, and so on.

Let yourself fully experience the sense of centeredness and focus before reengaging in the dance of life. Know that you are always only a breath away from centering.

THE GODDESSES

UZUME

LAUGHTER

Before the Rock Cave of Heaven
where Amaterasu Omi Kami, the
*   Sun Goddess*
had hidden her radiant face
where all the assembled Gods and
*   Goddesses had tried*
and failed
to lure her out
I stepped up to the Cave
with utmost seriousness
with grave determination
with proper decorum and a lofty mien
and with a bump and a bump and a bump bump bump bump
lifted my kimono and revealed myself in ways
that caused the mouths of the exalted ones
to water and fall open
Then I played puppet with my labia
and paid myself a little lip service
I heaved my breast over one shoulder
then the other over the other
and landed on my ass
with a bump and a bump and a bump bump bump bump
amidst the explosions of laughter and merriment
of the esteemed crowd

With breasts tied in a knot
my legs spread like a welcome mat
I called in the Spirits
and offered them my body . . .
but they refused to take it
The crowd howled and laughed as I continued my dance
till Amaterasu Omi Kami couldn't stand it any longer
and rushed out to see what was what
And thus did laughter
win the Sun Goddess from her dark cave
and bring light and warmth back into the world

Mythology

Uzume (pronounced *oo-zoo-may*), ancient Japan's shaman-Goddess, is credited as being the one to entice the Sun Goddess, **Amaterasu Omi Kami**, out of the cave where she had hidden. **Uzume** did a bawdy dance making fun of shamanic ritual. She exposed her breasts, she played with her genitals, amidst the howls of laughter of the deities assembled. So loud and enticing was the uproar she created, that **Amaterasu**'s curiosity got the better of her and she came out from her cave.

Meaning of the Card

Uzume begins her comic dance in your life to tell you it is time to nurture wholeness with laughter. Laughter causes us to relax, enables us to gain perspective, helps ease us through difficulties. Have you been taking life too seriously? When is the last time you had a good laugh? Are you able to laugh at yourself in a gentle

THE GODDESSES

way? Perhaps life is challenging you with such ferocity that you find it hard to see the humor in your present situation. **Uzume** says that wholeness is gained when you choose to laugh and see the humor in all of life's challenges.

Ritual Suggestion: Journey to Uzume

Find a time and a place when and where you will not be disturbed. Sit or lie comfortably with your spine straight and close your eyes. Take a deep breath and release it with a "ha, ha, ha." Take another deep breath and lift your shoulders up and down three times as you exhale. Take another deep breath and release it with a "ha, ha, ha" while moving your shoulders up and down as if you were having a good laugh. Take another deep breath and, as you exhale, see, sense, or feel the Rock Cave of Heaven. Take another deep breath and, as you release it, see yourself standing in front of the cave. Enter the cave. It is warm and pleasant. A small dancing sun appears before you to light your way through the darkness of the cave. You follow the dancing sun, enjoying its playfulness, becoming more relaxed, more at ease. The sun leads you to the light at the end of the cave where you step out into the Underworld. There you are met by **Uzume** who warmly welcomes you with a big smile. She takes you by the hand and leads you to a stage area with some cushions in front of it.

She sits on the cushions and gestures for you to do the same. She asks you what you need. You tell her you need help seeing the humor, the comedy, in a particular situation in your life. She agrees to help you. As you give her the details, the entire situation is played out before you on the stage. Once you have finished,

THE GODDESS ORACLE

she claps her hands twice and the entire scene is replayed as a comedy, complete with clowns and your favorite comic actors. It is very funny and you find yourself laughing and feeling light and carefree. When the scene is finished, **Uzume** claps and the scene vanishes. You thank **Uzume** and she asks you for a gift, which you give to her with an open heart. She escorts you back to the cave entrance where you are met by the dancing sun. You and the sun dance your way back through the cave, feeling energized, refreshed, revitalized, and as light as air. At the cave entrance you take a deep breath and come back to your body. Take another deep breath and, when ready, open your eyes. Welcome back!

VILA

SHAPE-SHIFTING

I dance from form to form
I shift from shape to shape
ever changing
ever expanding
ever becoming
I am flexibility
for by changing my form
I freely flow with all that comes
    my way
I am consciousness
for by shifting my shape
I gain an expanded awareness of what it is to Be

THE GODDESSES

I waltz a whirlwind
tango a tree
salsa a swan
or just plain fox-trot
My dance is an affinity with All
for I am able to become All in order to know All
Becoming All dissolves form
Knowing All creates Oneness
The illusion is that you have a separate shape

Mythology

Vila (pronounced *vee'lah*) is the eastern European name for the Goddess energy moving through the earth as nature. **Vily** (plural) are very protective of their terrain and use their arrows of death on those who trespass. They are consummate shape-shifters, able to change into animals such as snakes, swans, falcons, and horses. They love to play and dance. If contacted in the forest on a moonlit night, they might grant health, wealth, abundant crops or they might, if shown disrespect, dance the offender to death.

Meaning of the Card

Vila has come dancing into your life in her many forms to teach you to nourish wholeness by learning to shape-shift. Have you been too long in one form? Are you feeling stiff and stagnant, losing flexibility in your way of thinking and being? Or perhaps you feel that the human is the most important being in creation—that the rocks, trees, animals, earth, et cetera, are lesser forms. It is time to expand your awareness, to enhance your flexibility by gaining the perspective of other forms. **Vila** says the way to wholeness lies in experiencing the whole of creation.

Ritual Suggestion: Shape-shifting the Elements

Select a time and a place when and where you will not be disturbed. Stand, sit, or lie comfortably with your back straight and close your eyes. Take a deep breath and release it slowly, letting everything go with it. Take a deep breath into your womb, through your vagina. Feel the air fill your womb and then exit through your vagina. Keep breathing into your womb.

Stand facing the east and visualize, feel, sense the element air in whatever form you choose: a warm summer breeze, a windy March day. When you have a clear sense of the air, breathe it into your womb until your womb becomes the air. Let the air spread throughout your whole body, so that your body dissolves and you are the air. Allow yourself to experience oneness with the air until you are ready to move on. Then let the airy sensation recede into your womb and finally leave your body completely.

Facing south, get a strong sense, visual image, or feeling of fire. Is it a bonfire or a flickering candle? a forest fire or hearth fire? Focus on your image, then take it into your womb so that your womb becomes the fire. Let the fire gradually spread through your body so that you dissolve into the fire. Stay with the experience of being fire until it is time for you to return. Let the fire recede until it is only in your womb, then let the fire go completely.

Face the west and the element water. Sense, see, or feel a running stream, a calm clear pond, the immensity and power of the ocean, or a glass of water and focus on it. Then breathe it into your womb so that your womb becomes the water. Let it spread to the rest of your body so that your body dissolves and you become the water. Enjoy the experience of being water until you feel it is time to return. Gradually let the water recede till it is only in your womb, then release the water completely.

Face the north and the element of earth. Choose the image, sense, or feeling of earth that is appropriate for you—the mountains, jungle, forest, desert—and focus on it. Breathe it into your womb until your womb becomes one with the earth. Let the earth spread throughout your body until your body dissolves and you are the earth. Stay with that experience until you are ready to return. Gradually let the earth recede from your body until the earth is only in your womb, then release the earth completely. Take a deep breath and open your eyes. Welcome back to human form!

YEMAYA

SURRENDER

Come with your cares
come with your woes
come when life is joyful
come when life weighs you down
come when you take on too much
come when you are spread too thin
come when you are danced out

come when you seek renewal
all I ask when you come
is that you surrender to me
mother ocean
my watery womb waits to hold you
nurture you
birth you anew
when you let go and give over all to me

Mythology

Yemaya (pronounced *ee'mah-zha*) is a Santeria African-Caribbean Goddess of the sea, who gave birth to fourteen orishas, or spirits. Originally known as Ymoja, the West African Yoruban river mother, she also came to Brazil where she is known as Iamanja. At her celebration on the Summer Solstice, her worshippers arrive at her shorelines dressed in white and launch little boats loaded with flowers, candles, and gifts. Sometimes she accepts the offerings and prayers and sometimes she sends them back. It is said that those who come to Mother **Yemaya** and surrender to her find that their troubles dissolve in the waters of her embrace.

Meaning of the Card

Yemaya swimming into your life signals a time for surrender. Are you carrying more than you can handle comfortably? Do you think you must do it all by yourself? Have you come up against a wall and feel the only way to get to the other side is by breaking through? Surrender doesn't mean giving up; rather you are giving over, asking for assistance so you can do what you want to do.

THE GODDESSES

Wholeness is nurtured when you realize that the only way through some situations is to surrender and open to something greater. The act of surrendering is one of opening and trust. When we open and trust, we allow Goddess energy to work with us to achieve what we need.

Ritual Suggestion: Surrendering

You can do this ritual at the ocean or another body of water, or you can do this as a journey in imagination.

Prepare yourself by centering (you may want to see **Tara**: *Centering,* pp. 168–170). Take a deep breath and bring your awareness to your womb. Breathe in and out from your vulva. When you are ready, slowly and reverently enter the water while calling out to **Yemaya** to meet you. Find a place where you can float on your back in a safe and comfortable way. Feel **Yemaya** surrounding and supporting you. Let yourself go into her embrace.

You can experience the total embrace of **Yemaya** by physically surrendering to her or you can give over to **Yemaya** an aspect of your life with which you need assistance. Do you need help with your finances or love life or job hunt or search for housing? As the water washes over your body, as you float, **Yemaya** rinses you of all the burdens you carry. Let her take them from you. Give them to her willingly. See, sense, or feel yourself handing them over to her with relief and certainty that all will be taken care of. Let yourself go into the immensity of the ocean.

When you feel ready to return, thank **Yemaya** for your time with her. Then head back to the shore, feeling lighter, more vital, and clear. Welcome back!

SIBYL

Sibyl was the name given to the most renowned female prophets in ancient Persia, Libya, Delphi, Samos, Cimmeria, Erythraea, Tibur, Marpessus, Phrygia, and Cumae. Whether seated over noxious vapors from a crack in the earth, or buried deep in the silence and seclusion of her cave, Sibyl would utter her prophecies in trance or write them on leaves which were later dispersed by the wind if no one came to collect them. Although often esoteric and in need of further interpretation to be understood, Sibyl with her gift of prophecy, linked her people to the Divine.

As seen in the smoke
past the long ages of time
I have waited for you
Waited and known you would come
The prophecies I write are no longer on leaves
to be scattered, unclaimed, by the wind
nor am I the only voice of the Goddess
I have sat and waited
and now you are here
Take my bowl
gaze into the swirling smoke
soon you will hear Her voice
my gift of prophecy I give to you
to do with as you will
It is time that all women are sibyls
and that we all serve the Goddess

PART THREE

THE CARDS

THE GODDESS ORACLE

PAGE	GODDESS	QUALITY
21	Amaterasu	Beauty
23	Aphrodite	Love
26	Artemis	Selfhood
28	Baba Yaga	Wild Woman
31	Bast	Play
34	Blodeuwedd	Betrayal
38	Brigid	Inspiration
40	Cerridwen	Death and Rebirth
44	Changing Woman	Cycles
47	Coatlicue	Grief
50	Corn Woman	Nourishment
53	Demeter	Feelings/Emotions
56	Durga	Boundaries
59	Eostre	Growth
62	The Erinyes	Crisis
65	Eurynome	Ecstasy
68	Freya	Sexuality
72	Gyhldeptis	Synthesis
76	Hathor	Pleasure
78	Hecate	Crossroads
82	Hestia	Hearth/Home
84	Inanna	Embracing the Shadow
87	Isis	Mothering
91	Ix Chel	Creativity

THE CARDS

Ritual Suggestion	Culture/Country
Beauty Bath	Japan
Holding Space	Mediterranean
Taking Yourself Back	Mediterranean
Retrieving Your Wild Woman	Slavic
Playtime with **Bast**	Egypt
Journey to **Blodeuwedd**	Wales
Journey to **Brigid**	Celtic
Cerridwen's Cauldron	Wales
Celebrating Your Cycles	Navajo/Apache
Drumming Your Grief	Aztec
Sacred Eating	Southwestern indigenous aboriginals and pueblo peoples; the Arikara, Pawnee, Cheyenne, Mandan, Hidatsa, Abnaki, Cherokee, and Huron
Saying What Is So	Mediterranean
Sacred Circle of Self	India
Growth	Northern Europe
The Cocoon	Mediterranean
Dancing with **Eurynome**	Mediterranean
Making Love with the Elements	Northern Europe
Feasting in **Gyhldeptis**'s Festival House	Tlingit and Haida
The Pleasure Break	Egypt
Hecate's Journey of Perspective	Mediterranean
Coming Home	Mediterranean
Journey to Meet Your Shadow	Sumer
Journey to **Isis**	Egypt
Ix Chel's Energy Web	Mayan

Page	Goddess	Quality
94	Kali	Fear
97	Kuan Yin	Compassion
100	Lady of Beasts	Relationship
104	Lakshmi	Abundance
106	Lilith	Power
111	Maat	Justice
113	Maeve	Responsibility
117	Maya	Illusion
120	Minerva	Beliefs
123	Morgan le Faye	Rhythms
126	Nu Kua	Order
128	Nut	Mystery
131	Oshun	Sensuality
133	Oya	Change
136	Pachamama	Healing/Wholing/Holy
138	Pele	Awakening
141	Rhiannon	Doubt
144	Sedna	Victim
147	Sekhmet	Anger and Rage
150	Shakti	Energy
155	Sheila Na Gig	Opening
158	Sophia	Wisdom
160	Sphinx	Challenge
164	Sulis	Illness/Wellness
168	Tara	Centering
171	Uzume	Laughter
174	Vila	Shape-shifting
177	Yemaya	Surrender

THE CARDS

Ritual Suggestion	Culture/Country
Meeting Your Fear	India
Journey to **Kuan Yin**	China
Creating Win-Win Situations	Sumer, Crete, India
Flowing with **Lakshmi**	India
Cord-cutting Ceremony	South-west Asia
Handing Over to **Maat** for Justice	Egypt
Owning Dance	Ireland
Parting the Veils of Illusion	India
What's in My Attic?	Roman & Etruscan
Journey to Avalon	Wales
Journey to **Nu Kua**	China
Nut's Embrace	Egypt
The Bath	Santeria, Brazil, Macumba, Yoruba
Enlisting Change as Your Ally	Santeria, Brazil, Macumba, Yoruba
Opening to **Pachamama**	Peru, Bolivia
The Volcano	Hawaii
Doubt Alchemy	Wales
Dancing Your Victim	Inuit
Dancing with **Sekhmet**	Egypt
Cosmic Chakra Orgasm	India
Creating Opening	Ireland
Connecting with Your Inner **Sophia**	South-west Asia
Meeting Challenge Face-to-Face	Egypt, Mediterranean
Recalling and Rebuilding Your Inner Fire	Ancient Britain
Meeting **Tara** Through the Breath	India & Tibet
Journey to **Uzume**	Japan
Shape-shifting the Elements	Eastern Europe
Surrendering	Santeria, Brazil, Macumba, Yoruba

BIBLIOGRAPHY

Allen, Paula Gunn. *Grandmothers of the Light: A Medicine Woman's Sourcebook,* Boston: Beacon Press, 1991.

Ann, Martha, and Dorothy Myers Imel. *Goddesses in World Mythology: A Biographical Dictionary,* New York: Oxford University Press, 1993.

Blair, Nancy. *Amulets of the Goddess: Oracle of Ancient Wisdom,* Oakland, California: Wingbow Press, 1993.

Blum, Ralph. *The Book of Runes: A Handbook for the Use of an Ancient Oracle: The Viking Runes,* New York: Oracle Books, St. Martin's Press, 1982.

Bradshaw, John. *Homecoming: Reclaiming and Championing Your Inner Child,* New York: Bantam Books, 1990.

Caldecott, Moyra. *Women in Celtic Myth: Tales of Extraordinary Women from the Ancient Celtic Tradition,* Rochester, Vermont: Destiny Books, 1992.

Crowley, Vivianne. *Wicca: The Old Religion in the New Age,* Wellingborough, U.K.: The Aquarian Press, 1989.

Estés, Clarissa Pinkola. *Women Who Run with the Wolves: Myths and Stories of the Wild Woman Archetype,* New York: Ballantine Books, 1992.

George, Demetra. *Mysteries of the Dark Moon: The Healing Power of the Dark Goddess,* San Francisco: HarperSanFrancisco, 1992.

Gleason, Judith. *Oya: In Praise of the Goddess,* Boston: Shambhala, 1987.

Graves, Robert. *The White Goddess: A Historical Grammar of Poetic Myth,* New York: Farrar, Straus and Giroux, 1979.

BIBLIOGRAPHY

—*The Greek Myths,* vols. 1 & 2, New York: Penguin Books, 1960.

Jamal, Michele. *Deerdancer: The Shapeshifter Archetype in Story and in Trance,* New York: Arkana, 1995.

Johnson, Buffie. *Lady of the Beasts: The Goddess and Her Sacred Animals,* Rochester, Vermont: Inner Traditions International, 1994.

Johnson, Robert A. *Ecstasy: Understanding the Psychology of Joy,* San Francisco: HarperSanFrancisco, 1989.

Lerner, Harriet Goldhor. *The Dance of Anger: A Woman's Guide to Changing the Patterns of Intimate Relationships,* New York: HarperCollins, 1989.

Liedloff, Jean. *The Continuum Concept: Allowing Human Nature to Work Successfully,* Reading, Massachusetts: Addison-Wesley Publishing Company, 1985.

Matthews, Caitlin. *Sophia: Goddess of Wisdom,* London: Mandala, 1991.

Monaghan, Patricia. *The Book of Goddesses & Heroines,* St. Paul, Minnesota: Llewellyn Publications, 1993.

Mookerjee, Ajit. *Kali: The Feminine Force,* New York: Destiny Books, 1988.

Morgan, Fiona. *Daughters of the Moon Tarot,* Sebastopol, California: Daughters of the Moon, 1986.

Mountainwater, Shekhinah. *Ariadne's Thread: A Workbook of Goddess Magic,* Freedom, California: The Crossing Press, 1991.

Murdock, Maureen. *The Heroine's Journey: Woman's Quest for Wholeness,* Boston & London: Shambhala, 1990.

Noble, Vicki. *Motherpeace: A Way to the Goddess through Myth, Art, and Tarot,* San Francisco: HarperSanFrancisco, 1994.

Paris, Ginette. *Pagan Meditations: Aphrodite, Hestia, Artemis,* translated by Gwendolyn Moore, Dallas: Spring Publications, Inc., 1986.

Pollack, Rachel. *Shining Woman Tarot,* Wellingborough, U.K.: The Aquarian Press, 1992.

Sams, Jamie and David Carson. *Medicine Cards: The Discovery of Power through the Ways of Animals,* Santa Fe, New Mexico: Bear & Company, 1988.

Siegel, Bernie S., M.D., *Love, Medicine & Miracles,* New York: Harper Perennial, 1990.

Starhawk. *The Spiral Dance: A Rebirth of the Ancient Religion of the Great Goddess,* San Francisco: Harper & Row, 1979.

Stewart, R.J. *Celtic Gods, Celtic Goddesses, London:* Blandford Press, 1990.

Stone, Merlin. *Ancient Mirrors of Womanhood: A Treasury of Goddess and Heroine Lore from around the World,* Boston: Beacon Press, 1990.

—*When God Was a Woman,* New York: Harcourt Brace Jovanovich, 1976.

Wanless, James. *Voyager Tarot: Way of the Great Oracle,* Carmel, California: Merrill-West Publishing, 1989.

Walker, Barbara G. *The Woman's Encyclopedia of Myths and Secrets,* New York: Harper & Row, 1983.

—*The Woman's Dictionary of Symbols & Sacred Objects,* San Francisco: Harper & Row, 1988.

Weed, Susun S. *Wise Woman Herbal: Healing Wise,* Woodstock, New York: Ash Tree Publishing, 1989.

Wing, R. L. *The I Ching Workbook,* New York: Doubleday & Company, Inc., 1979.